AMERICAN ★ HISTORY

The SALEM WITCH TRIALS

A Crisis in Puritan New England

By Tanya Dellaccio

Portions of this book originally appeared in
The Salem Witch Trials by Don Nardo.

LUCENT
PRESS

Published in 2017 by
Lucent Press, an Imprint of Greenhaven Publishing, LLC
353 3rd Avenue
Suite 255
New York, NY 10010

Designer: Deanna Paternostro
Editor: Katie Kawa

Cataloging-in-Publication Data

Names: Dellaccio, Tanya.
Title: The Salem witch trials: a crisis in Puritan New England / Tanya Dellaccio.
Description: New York : Lucent Press, 2017. | Series: American history | Includes index.
Identifiers: ISBN 9781534560390 (library bound) | ISBN 9781534560406 (ebook)
Subjects: LCSH: Trials (Witchcraft)--Massachusetts--Salem--Juvenile literature. | Witchcraft--Massachusetts--Salem--History--17th century--Juvenile literature. | Witch hunting--Massachusetts--Salem--History--17th century--Juvenile literature.
Classification: LCC KFM2478.8.W5 D45 2017 | DDC 345.744'50288--dc23

CPSIA compliance information: Batch #CW17KL: For further information contact Greenhaven Publishing LLC, New York, New York at 1-844-317-7404.

Please visit our website, www.greenhavenpublishing.com. For a free color catalog of all our high-quality books, call toll free 1-844-317-7404 or fax 1-844-317-7405.

Contents

Foreword

The United States is a relatively young country. It has existed as its own nation for more than 200 years, but compared to nations such as China that have existed since ancient times, it is still in its infancy. However, the United States has grown and accomplished much since its birth in 1776. What started as a loose confederation of former British colonies has grown into a major world power whose influence is felt around the globe.

How did the United States manage to develop into a global superpower in such a short time? The answer lies in a close study of its unique history. The story of America is unlike any other—filled with colorful characters, a variety of exciting settings, and events too incredible to be anything other than true.

Too often, the experience of history is lost among the basic facts: names, dates, places, laws, treaties, and battles. These fill countless textbooks, but they are rarely compelling on their own. Far more interesting are the stories that surround those

basic facts. It is in discovering those stories that students are able to see history as a subject filled with life—and a subject that says as much about the present as it does about the past.

The titles in this series allow readers to immerse themselves in the action at pivotal historical moments. They also encourage readers to discuss complex issues in American history—many of which still affect Americans today. These include racism, states' rights, civil liberties, and many other topics that are in the news today but have their roots in the earliest days of America. As such, readers are encouraged to think critically about history and current events.

Each title is filled with excellent tools for research and analysis. Fully cited quotations from historical figures, letters, speeches, and documents provide students with firsthand accounts of major events. Primary sources also bring authority to the text. Sidebars highlight these quotes and primary sources, as well as interesting figures and events. Annotated bibliographies allow students to locate and evaluate sources for further information on the subject.

A deep understanding of America's past is necessary to understand its present and its future. Sometimes you have to look back to see how to best move forward, and that's certainly true when writing the next chapter in the American story.

Setting the Scene:

1233
Pope Gregory IX establishes the medieval Inquisition, which eventually hunts down witches.

1484
Pope Innocent VIII declares in an edict that witches are real.

1534
King Henry VIII separates England from Roman Catholicism, creating the Church of England.

| 1233 | 1431 | 1484 | 1492 | 1534 | 1607 | 1630 |

1431
The Inquisition arrests, tries, and executes the French warrior-maiden Joan of Arc for witchcraft.

1607
English settlers land at Jamestown, Virginia, the first of England's American colonies.

1492
Sailing for Spain, Italian-born mariner Christopher Columbus lands in the West Indies, initiating a great age of global exploration.

1630
A group of Puritans sail with John Winthrop to settle the Massachusetts Bay Colony.

A Timeline

1692
Twenty people are executed and hundreds are imprisoned as the famous witch trials take place in Salem.

1851
Nathaniel Hawthorne, a descendant of one of the prosecutors in the witch trials, writes *The House of the Seven Gables*.

1992
A memorial is dedicated in Salem, Massachusetts, in honor of all of the victims of the Salem witch trials.

2001
Massachusetts clears the charges of five women that were executed during the Salem witch trials.

1692	1711	1776	1851	1952	1992	2001	2016

1776
England's colonies in North America, including Massachusetts, declare their independence, creating the United States.

2016
A research team confirms the location of the hangings in Massachusetts during the witch trials.

1711
The Massachusetts government grants financial restitution to the families of some of the accused Salem witches.

1952
American playwright Arthur Miller writes *The Crucible* about the Salem witch trials.

Introduction

A HISTORY BASED ON FALSE ACCUSATIONS

There are often situations in history in which important, calculated decisions were made in order to seek the greater good. These decisions—from sending a country to war to something more isolated, such as establishing law practices for an individual community—are, at the time, considered the best option for the greater good. When it comes to the case of the Salem witch trials, the people of Salem reacted as best they could to the situation that arose. In the 1600s, societies sought out explanations for unusual situations to the best of their knowledge. However, without proper physical or mental examinations available to them, the decisions they made led to one of the worst cases of mass hysteria in history.

People began settling in Salem, a village in present-day Massachusetts, around the 1620s. This village was inhabited mainly by Puritans, English Protestants who wanted to purify religious practices. One day in January 1692, two young girls in the community began exhibiting strange behavior, including seizure-like fits. The community was not medically advanced, however, and these behaviors resulted in severe confusion and misunderstanding. The community's final explanation for the behavior was that a witch was causing the young girls physical suffering by some profound act of worshipping the devil. Since the two girls were only 11 and 9 years old, they accepted their diagnoses and continued to portray themselves as victims of witchcraft, pointing fingers and accusing members of the community of being witches. These accusations, stemming from 2 young girls, sparked the witch hunt that killed 20 people and, through false accusations, ruined the lives of several others.

How could such a travesty of justice

The trials of the accused witches represented the height of the hysteria that surrounded Salem in 1692.

have occurred in what was then considered a civilized society? After all, witches—when defined as followers of Satan who use evil, supernatural powers to do his bidding—do not exist.

At the time of the Salem witch trials, a majority of people in Europe and its recently founded colonies in North America were convinced that witches were real. In fact, witchcraft was widely believed in throughout the world in that particular time period. The arrest, prosecution, imprisonment, and execution of suspected witches in Salem were, therefore, the result of widespread ignorance,

superstition, and fear. Since the witch trials quickly became so widely known, documentation and factual accounts of several parties involved have been preserved and passed down to further educate later societies on the tragic event.

"Fear, Hatred, and Envy"

The sordid and tragic events of the trials in Salem are, historically speaking, noteworthy in their own right. They constitute one of the most extreme, fascinating, and often-documented incidents in American history. However, this localized outbreak of contagious fear and violence is also important because it sheds light on other similar cases of mass hysteria, persecution, and grave injustice in the human saga. According to Frances Hill, one of the leading modern scholars of the Salem witch trials, these troubling incidents

> provide an astonishingly clear and instructive model of the universal and timeless processes by which groups of human beings instigate, justify, and escalate persecution … Because the numbers of people involved in the Salem witch-hunt and the timescale of events, were on a small scale, the steps are easy to trace by which a few deranged, destructive human beings led ordinary mortals down the dark paths of fear, hatred, and envy to demonize and destroy innocent victims. When those steps are understood, the recurrent persecutions in human history, whether, ethnic, religious, political, or superstitious, become less hard to comprehend.[1]

In fact, the "dark paths of fear, hatred and envy" that caused the persecution of suspected witches in Salem were by no means new to the inhabitants of Massachusetts and their European ancestors. Those dark paths had formed long before as a set of fear-based religious and social beliefs about witches. A brief examination of these beliefs reveals the roots of the strange, twisted mindset that gripped those who sought out and killed suspected witches in Salem in the late 1600s.

At that time, Europe had only recently emerged from its medieval era (roughly spanning the years AD 400 to 1500), and a number of common folk beliefs and myths of that period were still widely accepted, including those relating to witches.

In medieval times in Europe, witches were generally seen as women—but also sometimes men—who did the bidding of the devil. It was thought that witches engaged in acts with the devil or with demons; flew through the sky; turned themselves into wolves, bats, and other animals; became invisible at will; and harassed or corrupted average people.

Pope Innocent VIII's Influence

Although people all over Europe readily believed in witches, for several centuries, these supernatural beings were viewed as a relatively minor threat to society. Even when Pope Gregory IX established the papal Inquisition to combat heresy in the Roman Catholic Church and authorized the killing of suspected witches in the 1200s, few were hunted down and executed in the two centuries that followed. The situation changed, however, and much for the worse, after Pope Innocent VIII released an edict in 1484. It stated in no uncertain terms that witches were real. Because the Church then held sway over the minds of most Europeans, large numbers of people took the pope's words

Pope Innocent's view on witches greatly influenced the events that transpired in Salem, Massachusetts, in 1692.

The portrayal of witches in the Malleus Maleficarum *was widely believed by many* because of the intellectual standing of the monks who wrote it.

quite seriously. Those few who doubted that witches were real were silenced by the fear of being branded a heretic (someone who, in thought or deed, goes against the teachings of God and the Church).

To reinforce Pope Innocent's tough stance against witches, in 1486, two German Dominican monks and inquisitors for the Inquisition, James Sprenger and Heinrich Kramer, published the *Malleus Maleficarum*, or *The Hammer of Witches*. This volume listed the supernatural acts performed by witches and told how witches caused disease, destroyed crops, and kidnapped and ate children. At the time, monks were among the few educated people in Europe. Citizens tended to assume that a book written by monks and approved by the pope must be both righteous and factual. Not surprisingly, considering the cultural backwardness of the times, no one seemed to notice the authors' narrow-mindedness, hatred of women, and lack of sympathy for normal human feelings. The following passage from *Malleus Maleficarum* explains why more women than men are witches and is typical of beliefs at that time:

> Now the wickedness of women is spoken of in [the Bible, which says that] … all wickedness is but little to the wickedness of a woman … [W]omen are naturally more impressionable, and more ready to receive the influence of a disembodied spirit … they have slippery tongues, and are unable to conceal from their fellow women those things which by evil arts they know;

> and, since they are weak, they find an easy and secret manner of vindicating themselves by witchcraft … We may add … that since they are feebler both in mind and body, it is not surprising that they should come more under the spell of witchcraft.[2]

To understand how an entire community could cause such mass hysteria, we must first look at the beliefs and teachings of those who influenced them. This passage helps show the mindset of the people in power in these times. Their influence was, of course, taken very seriously and almost always blindly obeyed.

Forced Confessions Lead to Mass Hysteria

Due to Sprenger and Kramer's book, sermons based on it, and other church-sanctioned ravings about witches, a wave of mass hysteria about the threat of witches began to sweep over Europe. In the two centuries that followed, hunts, trials, and executions of witches occurred in Germany, Italy, France, Sweden, Switzerland, Spain, and other lands. According to scholar James A. Haught, "Most of the victims were old women whose [stooped posture, wrinkled skin, and seemingly odd personal habits] roused the suspicions of neighbors. Others were young, pretty women. Some were men. Many in continental Europe were simply citizens whose names were shrieked out by torture victims when commanded to identify witches."[3]

In fact, torture was a regular feature

One form of torture used on an accused witch was dunking them in and out of water, hoping to get a confession out of them.

of the persecution and prosecution of suspected witches. The authorities inflicted gruesome physical abuses on the victims, in part to get them to confess to practicing witchcraft, and also to divulge the names of other witches. Generally, the suspects were stripped of their clothes, and then their hair was shaved to look for any devil's marks on their skin or even a demon hiding in their hair. Sometimes, their fingernails were pulled out. It was common to apply red-hot metal tongs to the victim's body and to stretch the person's body on a rack, which would dislocate the joints. Another form of both punishment and confession was trial by water, in which the suspected witch would be dunked in water on a stool until they confessed or were bound and thrown into a pond. The belief was that the suspect would sink if a witch but float if innocent. This form of confession was banned in many countries in the Middle Ages and came back in the 1600s. The results of these cruelties were predictable; as Haught wrote, "Virtually every mangled and broken victim confessed—and was executed on the basis of the confession."[4]

The total number of European women and men who were tortured and killed on suspicion of being witches is unknown. Estimates by modern scholars range from about 100,000 to as many as 9 million. Eventually, this horrible travesty ran its course. Arrests of suspected witches had dramatically declined in number by the late 1600s and early 1700s, partly because of the more rational thinking that accompanied the rise of modern science in those years.

Thus, the Salem witch trials, which took place in a European outpost, represented one of the last gasps of the witch mania that had so long infected Europe. Though they happened far across the sea from the sites of the medieval witch hunts, the shameful incidents in Salem were, in a number of ways, linked to those earlier travesties of justice. The Salem witch trials "could never have happened," Hill pointed out, "if the supernatural beliefs the Puritans had brought with them from England … had not retained their conviction and power right through the seventeenth century."[5] Only after the execution of several people in Salem did reason settle amongst the community and diminish the concept of witchcraft as a real and punishable offense.

Chapter One

THE STRONG BELIEFS THAT LED TO CHAOS

The strong and steady beliefs among the Puritans provided much of the driving force in the infamous Salem witch trials. These beliefs, which followed what they believed to be the teachings of God very closely, gave people in 17th-century Salem a false outlook on how many situations should be handled. When the witch trials began, there is no doubt that the heightened sense of religion among the community members created an atmosphere that readily accepted the idea of devil worshippers practicing witchcraft.

Much of everyday life in Salem could be defined as very simplistic. The luxuries of technology and entertainment were unavailable in the 1600s, and members of the community often took on specific roles in order to further the functionality of the village itself. These simplistic roles often were tasks of vital necessity, as a woman's job was often cooking, cleaning, and taking care of the home, while a man's job was often something that utilized his strength. All members of the community were expected to attend church services, while living every moment of the day under a firm understanding that each decision was to be made with the consideration that God was watching them closely and judging them for any sinful or unholy act.

It is important to remember these common beliefs amongst the Puritans of Salem when discussing the beginning of the witch trials. The common core of their belief system was to disregard individuality and blame the devil for any act or situation that was out of the ordinary. These ideals proved crucial in the trials' unfolding and the community's acceptance to blame witchcraft for the citizens' shortcomings.

The History of Puritanism

The religious sect that came to be known as Puritanism emerged from the turmoil surrounding the early years of the Church of England. Before the 16th century, England, like other European lands, was a Catholic country that, in religious matters, recognized the authority of the pope in Rome. That situation changed quite suddenly and drastically in the 1530s. When the religious authorities in Rome refused to grant King Henry VIII a divorce, he angrily and boldly separated his country from the Catholic Church. The result was the formation of the Church of England, a Protestant denomination of Christianity.

As time went on, the English monarchs and most of their subjects felt that their new church satisfactorily met their needs. However, a few of the more devout inhabitants of the country were not so

This image shows John Winthrop leading Puritans into Salem.

happy with the new religious climate. They came to view the new church as too liberal, permissive, and even corrupt. Because they desired to purify the church by taking it back to stricter, more fundamental Christian ideas and customs, they became known as Puritans.

It is not surprising that the Puritans quickly earned a reputation as troublemakers, especially to the reigning monarchs and high-ranking church leaders.

In the early 1600s, these leaders began to persecute the Puritans. In response, some of the Puritans fled to Holland, while one group of Puritans crossed the Atlantic Ocean in 1620 and established a colony at Plymouth, in what is now southern Massachusetts. The Plymouth Puritans came to be known as the Pilgrims.

Not long after the landfall at Plymouth, other Puritans arrived and settled in an area further north on the Massachusetts coast. In 1628, John Endecott, a Puritan leader, formally founded Salem, which grew into the first town in a large new colony—Massachusetts Bay. Other Puritans were soon drawn to this new North American outpost. John Winthrop, who became the first governor of the colony, led about 1,000 Puritans to Salem in 1630. However, because of overcrowding, many of these newcomers struck out on their own and

A Religion Rooted in Fear

The extreme degree of piety felt and displayed by the vast majority of colonial Puritans is partly revealed by the words of a sermon delivered by the early Puritan minister and governor John Winthrop in 1630:

> If we deal falsely with our God in this work we have undertaken and so cause him to withdraw his present help from us, we shall be made a story ... throughout the world. We shall open the mouths of enemies to speak evil of the ways of God ... There is now set before us life and good, death and evil in that we are commanded this day to love the Lord our God, and to love one another, to walk in his ways and to keep his Commandments ... and his laws ... But if our hearts shall turn away [from God] so that we will not obey [him] ... we shall surely perish.[1]

1. Quoted in Suzanne McIntire and William E. Burns, *Speeches in World History*, New York, NY: Facts on File, 2009, p. 143.

established new towns nearby, including Watertown, Medford, and Dorchester. The largest group of Puritans settled along the Charles River about 15 miles (24 km) south of Salem at a spot they named Boston. The Massachusetts Bay Colony grew rapidly, taking in almost 20,000 more Puritan immigrants by 1640.

An Inferior Village
Also established in the Massachusetts Bay Colony during this period was Salem Village, at first called Salem Farms. Salem Village was a separate entity from Salem Town. Located along the coast, Salem Town was a bustling port with a number of shops, large merchants' houses, and local government buildings. In contrast, Salem Village (which is now the small town of Danvers) consisted of a few scattered farms and farmhouses roughly clustered around the village center. That center

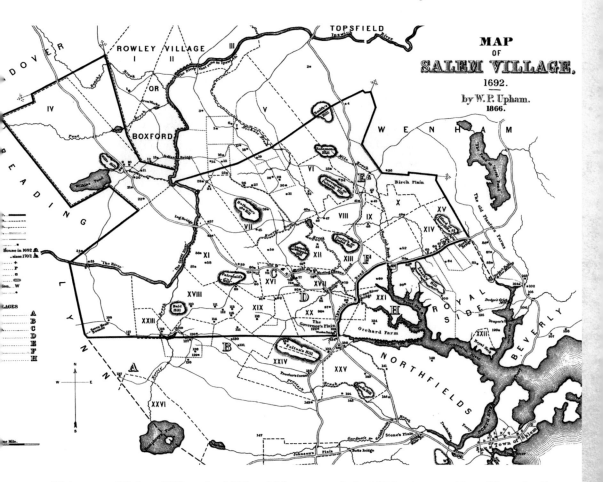

This map of Salem Village in 1692, which was made in 1866, gives an idea of how far the people in the community had to travel for everyday tasks.

eventually featured a meetinghouse, which doubled as a church, a parsonage (home for the local minister), a small tavern, and a few houses owned by local tradesmen. Beyond the village's cultivated fields stretched large expanses of uncharted forests inhabited by groups of Native Americans.

The remoteness of Salem Village from the other Puritan towns is illustrated by the fact that it took a person between two and three hours to walk from the village to Salem Town. The distance between them was about 5 miles (8 km), but travelers had to cross several small rivers and inlets. At first, this trip presented a major physical challenge to the residents of Salem Village. Before the meetinghouse was erected in the village center in 1672, every Sunday, they had to walk all the way to the church in Salem Town and back again.

This initial reliance on the church and other facilities in the town was not the only source of frustration to the inhabitants of Salem Village. For a long time, they had little say in running their village, which fell under the legal and political jurisdiction of Salem Town. The leaders of the town taxed the villagers and set the prices for crops and other items exported from the village to the town. The town's elders also appointed the village's constable and controlled the distribution of land parcels and the building of roads in the village. For years, village leaders repeatedly lodged complaints and petitions in an effort to gain more autonomy. However, it was not until 1752, long after the Salem witch trials had ended, that the village finally broke free and became the independent town of Danvers.

Practicing Puritanism in Uncomfortable Conditions

Even when the citizens of Salem Village got their own meetinghouse in 1672, no one viewed it as a luxury, partly because the Puritan ethic rejected the very idea of luxury or any form of personal pleasure. In fact, Puritan society vigorously promoted a simple existence, even when worshipping God. Like other Puritan meetinghouses, the one in Salem Village had no heat. Worshippers were allowed to bring blankets, but on the harshest winter days, these provided only minimal relief from the numbing cold. The summer, in contrast, brought a different sort of discomfort in the form of mosquitoes, flies, and ticks from a nearby swamp.

One could not avoid these conditions by choosing to stay home on Sunday. In Salem, as in other Puritan communities, attending church was mandated by law. Everyone, without exception, had to sit through a three-hour service on Sunday morning and a two-hour service on Sunday afternoon. The rest of the day was devoted to prayer, Bible reading, and other religious activities. Moreover, during the formal services, the worshippers were literally forced to pay attention to the minister—a tithing-man walked through the aisles

This is an example of what a Puritan church in the 1600s may have looked like.

and used his hand or a stick to prod anyone who fell asleep or tried to whisper something to his or her neighbor.

The strictness of Puritan laws and customs relating to religious worship was matched by the harsh manner in which society treated many of its members. The Puritans openly practiced what today are recognized as serious forms of discrimination and abuse. In general, society catered to the young, the strong, the wealthy, and the male. Women were seen as inferior, as were poor people, most elderly people (especially women), and handicapped people; of the latter, those born with severe birth defects were viewed as the devil's offspring.

The notion that women, particularly old women, were the most likely members of society to be witches was inherent in this social prejudice, a bias the Puritans inherited from the recent witch hunts in Europe.

Gender and class discrimination even invaded the church, where the wealthiest people got the best seats (in front, closest to the pulpit) and men and women sat in separate sections. Puritan teachings and ministers claimed that such social divisions and unequal treatment were God's will. With only very rare exceptions, no one dared to question this view.

Being Careful

These attitudes and practices show how thoroughly religious ideas and observances pervaded Salem and other Puritan areas in the Massachusetts Bay Colony. Indeed, God's will, good versus evil, and divine punishment were concepts that regularly spilled over from the church into all areas of society. The common belief was that nearly everything people did and said was somehow connected to God and had divine consequences of some kind. As historian Richard Weisman explained:

Crop failures, epidemics, Indian raids, and … other disasters were perceived not as accidents or as the mere logical [aspects] of wilderness living but rather as judgments rendered according to the moral failings of the community. As the national sins increased, so would the severity of divine afflictions. Insofar as God maintained his covenant with [Puritan society in] New England, the members would have clear and continuous guidelines regarding the extent of their progress toward or departure from the realization of communal goals.[6]

If the community was to thrive, therefore, people needed to be careful not to provoke or anger God in any way—no matter how slight. This is part of the reason the Puritans banned all forms of public entertainment, including dancing and going to the theater. They viewed such activities as frivolous, against God's will, and inspired by the devil. Even when worshippers sang hymns in church, they did so in a droning monotone because they believed that the expression of a catchy tune might bring the singers pleasure, and in their view, God frowned on all forms of pleasure. Living under the constraints of

Harsh punishment was very common in a Puritan community. Puritans believed that if you sinned, you must pay dearly for it.

Normal Behavior as a Criminal Offense

Like the Puritans' religious beliefs and practices, their legal system was extremely strict and harsh, recognizing a wide range of criminal offenses. Most of these are viewed today as mere personal faults or even as normal behavior. Among the many cases that came to court in Salem on a single day, June 27, 1664, were the following:

> Robert Goodell [is to be] fined for suffering his goat to go in his neighbor's cornfield. Alice George of Gloucester [is] to be whipped or fined for railing against [scolding] Mr. Blynman, "calling him [a] wicked wretch," ... Michael Lambert of Lynn [got] drunk. [He later] confessed that he had drank three or four cups of sack [liquor] ... Daniel Ray, for trespass of his horses, cows and hogs in North field to his neighbor's ... James George, servant to William Cantleburie, [is] to be whipped for often running away from his master.[1]

1. Quoted in Frances Hill, ed., *The Salem Witch Trials Reader*. New York, NY: Da Capo, 2000, pp. 35–36.

such a stern and authoritarian mindset, it was easy to conclude that anyone who veered from these rules was potentially an agent of the devil.

It was not only personal enjoyment that supposedly led to God's displeasure. Any sort of rule breaking or social nonconformity was seen as a threat to society, and the perpetrator was subject to public punishment. Among the common sins and crimes were failing to attend church, kissing in public, breaking an engagement to be married, and disagreeing with community leaders on any matter. One common punishment was to be tied to a post and whipped. Another was to sit for hours or days in the stocks, which were wooden frameworks that trapped a person's hands, feet, and head. Still another penalty was exile, as happened to Roger Williams; his offense was promoting the idea that people should be allowed to worship how and when they pleased. In 1635, he was banished and soon afterward, established a new colony farther south, in what is now Rhode Island. The harshest punishment in the Massachusetts Bay Colony was death, which was generally by hanging. This is how 19 of the 20 accused witches who were con-demned to be executed in Salem met their untimely end.

A Woman's Restrictions

The Puritans' strict religious beliefs, customs, laws, and punishments were not the only factors that were destined to contribute to the wholesale prose-cution of suspected witches in Salem. True, an unhealthy preoccupation with the devil and the ongoing strug-gle between the forces of good and evil made many of the town's inhabitants believe that witches might actually be living among them. However, no one would have been accused of witchcraft in the first place if it had not been for the strange behavior of a few local young people. They succeeded in making near-ly everyone in their society believe that they had been tormented and possessed by witches. Their personal fascination with the supernatural and the attention and notoriety they received when they underwent violent physical convulsions were key factors in the witch hysteria that gripped the town.

The fact that all of these young peo-ple were female is revealing. In Puritan society in general, and especially in the small, remote village of Salem, women had far fewer opportunities and outlets for personal expression and satisfaction than men had. In winter, scholar Mari-on L. Starkey writes, men were relieved of most of their more time-consuming farm chores and

they could take a musket into the for-est to shoot wild turkey, deer, and a marauding fox or wolf. Or they could fetch a line and hook, cut through the ice, and fish. Housebound, they could turn to the secondary trade that nearly every Puritan frontiersman practiced in his spare time. Some cobbled shoes. Some fashioned trays ... of goodsmell-ing wood ... Men and boys were not often idle, not often bored.[7]

However, women in Salem Village, especially younger women, led lives that can only be described as subservient, nar-row, restrictive, and monotonous in the extreme. They were far from idle, and they regularly did housework and farm chores. For them, though, life was nothing but work of a very repetitious nature with lit-tle or no element of novelty, creativity, or enjoyment. "For young girls still unspo-ken-for," Starkey points out, "winter was unrelieved drudgery."[8]

Today, people often speak of young people rebelling against their elders, a behavior that is expected and considered normal. However, young Puritans, par-ticularly young women, had no socially accepted way to rebel. Instead, they chan-neled their repressed natural feelings into other areas, particularly into excessive, overly dramatic displays of religious zeal. These might include swooning or faint-ing during Bible readings or sermons that described the sufferings of Jesus or repeating the same prayer over and over again for hours on end.

God-Fearing People

Eventually, several young women in Salem Village took such displays to a new level. They allowed their pent-up feelings and energies to pour out in the performance of seizure-like fits supposedly caused by the assaults of witches. Along with these turbulent episodes, the girls later received a sort of twisted gratification from the excitement of the witch trials they helped to bring about. In a way, Carol F. Karlsen, a historian at the University of Michigan, wrote, they became the central figures in a "social drama" in which

> the more attention they received, the more they dramatized their socially generated anguish and their internally generated desire to rebel. As the community looked on, their bodies expressed what they otherwise could not: that the enormous pressures put upon them to accept a religiously based, male-centered social order was more than they could bear. To accept the community's truth was to deny the self ... Their religious beliefs led the possessed finally to confirm the only reality their culture allowed, the reality articulated by their ministers ... There were only two kinds of women: godly women and witches.[9]

This stark contrast between good and evil, with no allowance for any area in between, was typical for Puritan society on the eve of the infamous witch trials. The residents of Salem Village, along with the residents of neighboring towns, had been led to believe by their ministers and elders that there were only two kinds of people. In the words of the Reverend Samuel Parris, who came to play a key role in the trials, one was either a "saint," which meant a good, God-fearing person, or a "devil," which was a sinner or witch. In a sermon delivered in March 1692, Parris declared:

> Christ knows who these devils are [in our church] ... Christ knows how many devils [walk] among us—whether one, or ten, or twenty, [and] also who they are: He knows us perfectly, [and] he knows those of us that are in the church, that we are either saints or devils; true believers, or hypocrites [and] dissembling Judases that would sell Christ [and] his kingdom to gratify [their sinful] lust.[10]

In a society so fear-ridden that its members readily believed these paranoid words, it would take only a tiny spark of suspicion to ignite a blaze of terror, hysteria, and injustice. That is exactly what happened in Salem Village early in 1692.

Chapter Two

A BLIND FOLLOWING

In January 1692, Elizabeth Parris and Abigail Williams sparked the beginning of one of the most well-known fits of hysteria in history. Both girls began having physical fits, similar to seizures. These fits seemed peculiar to their elders and other prominent community members. Society at the time did not consider that there could be a mental or physical diagnosis causing these fits. Instead, the community made the decision that the devil was to blame for their ailments, and he was making other members of the community perform witchcraft.

If this happened in modern times, the situation would have most likely resulted in a medical diagnosis of something physically or mentally being wrong with the girls. However, the Puritans of Salem came to the conclusion that whatever was happening to the girls was completely unholy, and without question, the rest of the community blindly followed.

The idea of witchcraft did not stem from the minds of the people of Salem; it was passed down from several previous altercations in which women in colonial New England were persecuted for the use of witchcraft.

One of the biggest proponents of the idea was Cotton Mather, a minister of a local church. Mather's views on religion and serving God were very firm. He believed that no one was safe from punishments for their sins. In his book, *A Token for the Children of New England*, he discussed the acceptance of punishment and death for children, as well as adults. This idea, that a young child could be so sinful as to require the punishment of death, shows how this man could believe that an unholy act was taking place and how quick he was to enforce punishment. His remembrance of the previous incidents of witchcraft persecution only added to the community's

Cotton Mather's strict views on religion and extreme punishment led to the wrongful executions of many accused witches.

affirmation that this was indeed what was occurring to these two young girls.

With Mather being a point of influence in Salem, it is no surprise that his ideas were accepted without question. His beliefs and the beliefs of those in his company were a large part of the hysteria that ensued.

The First Trials

Among the prior witch hunts that Mather and others involved in the Salem trials remembered was the earliest recorded arrest and execution of a colonial Puritan for witchcraft. Anne Hibbins of Boston was the sister of a colonial governor, Richard Bellingham, and the wife of a prominent merchant, William Hibbins. Unfortunately for Mrs. Hibbins, she earned a reputation for having a temper and speaking her mind, which Puritans believed were unholy traits. In particular, she was chastised on several occasions for raising her voice to and arguing with men.

Not long after her husband died in 1654, Anne Hibbins mentioned to her neighbors that she believed people had been talking about her. Her neighbors then reported her to the authorities. They promptly arrested her and claimed that the only way she could have known she was the subject of someone else's conversation was by exercising evil powers, specifically the supernatural abilities attributed to witches. A jury found her guilty, and she was executed in 1656.

Another witch trial and execution occurred in Hartford, now the capital of the state of Connecticut, six years later. It is important to note that the supposed victim of witchcraft in this case, Ann Cole, exhibited many of the same physical symptoms—including convulsions—later displayed by Elizabeth Parris and Abigail Williams in Salem. About Cole's disturbing symptoms, Increase Mather, a prominent Puritan minister and Cotton Mather's father, wrote,

> She was and is accounted a person of real piety and integrity. Nevertheless, in the Year 1662 … she was taken with very strange Fits, wherein her Tongue was [caused] by a [demon] to express things which she [herself] knew nothing of. Sometimes the [evil ravings] would [go on] for a considerable time.[11]

It did not take the local authorities long to arrest another Hartford woman, Rebecca Greensmith, and charge her with using evil powers to afflict poor Ann Cole. For reasons unknown, Greensmith confessed to being a witch. Perhaps she was tortured and, to avoid further agony, said whatever her tormentors wanted her to. In any case, Increase Mather reported that she described how

> the Devil first appeared to her in the form of a deer or fawn, skipping about her, wherewith she was not much [afraid], and that by degrees he became very familiar, and at last would talk with her … And that the Witches had Meetings at a place not far from her House; and that some appeared in one shape, and others in another; and one came flying amongst them in the shape of a Crow.[12]

Based on this confession, Rebecca Greensmith was executed, along with her husband, whom the authorities concluded had helped her commit evil deeds. Another case in which Puritan children suffered fits very similar to those of Elizabeth Parris and Abigail Williams took place in Boston in 1688. Four of the six children of a reputable mason named John Goodwin were affected, as later told by Cotton Mather:

The children were tormented just in the same part of their bodies all at the same time together ... [Likewise] their pains and sprains were swift like lightning, yet when the ... neck, or the hand, or the back of one was racked, so it was at that instant with [the others] too ... Sometimes they would be deaf, sometimes dumb, and sometimes blind ... Their tongues would be drawn down their throats ... [and] their heads would be twisted almost [around].[13]

Hanging was a common style of execution for people found guilty of witchcraft in Puritan communities.

The children blamed their laundress, Mary Glover, for their strange afflictions. The authorities, who already viewed Mrs. Glover with suspicion because they believed she was scandalous, agreed that she was the culprit. They tried her as a witch and hanged her.

Tituba's Caribbean Magic

There was, therefore, ample precedent in New England's Puritan communities for young people having physical convulsions and blaming them on supposed witches. Moreover, it is likely no coincidence that the first children to suffer such fits in Salem lived in the house of the local minister. Reverend Samuel Parris had moved to Salem from Boston in 1689, only about a year after the execution of Mary Glover. Parris and the members of his family—including his wife, three children, and niece, Abigail Williams—were surely well acquainted with Glover's trial and the debilitating physical symptoms supposedly suffered by John Goodwin's children. The fact that 9-year-old Elizabeth Parris, nicknamed "Betty," and 11-year-old Abigail knew about the Goodwin children and might have copied their symptoms, either consciously or unconsciously, is often overlooked in modern studies of the Salem witch trials.

Another factor that made the Parris household a likely place for strange and seemingly supernatural behaviors to occur was the presence of two slaves. When they moved from Boston to Salem, the Parris family brought along John Indian and his wife, Tituba. John worked in the fields and took care of the family's livestock. Tituba cleaned the house and did laundry and other chores. She also cared for and entertained the Parris children on a regular basis because Mrs. Parris was often sick.

Like other young Puritan girls, Betty and Abigail were often bored, particularly in the winter months, and welcomed the attention of Tituba. The girls frequently spent hours at a time listening to the older woman tell stories about life in the Caribbean. It was only natural for Tituba to include information about magic, since both black and white magic were features of Caribbean island culture. (Black magic consisted of spells intended to hurt other people; white magic was thought to bring good fortune or to reveal glimpses of the future.) Thus, the presence of Tituba in the household almost ensured that the Parris children would be exposed to knowledge of the supernatural.

The exact sequence of events leading from Betty and Abigail's listening to stories from and playing games with Tituba to the girls' first experiences with seizure-like fits is unclear. What seems certain is that at some point in the winter of 1692, Tituba and the girls played a game that supposedly could reveal certain future events. Specifically, it was thought to predict the professions of the girls' future husbands.

One played the game by dropping an egg white into a glass of water. If the egg white formed a shape that looked like a hammer, it

This illustration of Tituba telling stories to a group of Puritan girls is from the 19th century.

indicated that the future husband would be a carpenter. Various other shapes stood for other professions.

Playing such a game today would likely be seen as harmless fun. However, in 17th-century Puritan society, such games were forbidden because magic was thought to be the devil's work. Thus, Betty and Abigail were aware that what they were doing was wrong in the eyes of their parents and society, yet as children with natural

Bitten by a "Witch"

Deodat Lawson, who served as minister in Salem Village before Reverend Samuel Parris assumed that post, later described a disturbing incident involving one of the afflicted girls, Mary Walcott:

On the nineteenth day of March last, I went to Salem Village, and lodged at Nathaniel Ingersoll's [tavern] near to the minister, Mr. Parris's house, and presently, after I came into my lodging, Captain [Jonathan] Walcott's daughter, Mary [age seventeen] came to Lt. Ingersoll's and spoke to me but suddenly after, as she stood by the door, [she] was bitten so that she cried out of her wrist [being bitten] and looking on it with a candle, we saw apparently the marks of teeth both upper and lower set, on each side of her wrist.[1]

1. Quoted in Elaine G. Breslaw, ed., *Witches of the Atlantic World: An Historical Reader and Primary Sourcebook*, New York, NY: New York University Press, 2000, pp. 389–390.

urges to experiment and rebel, they did it anyway. In fact, they told some of their closer friends about their secret games, and Tituba's circle of young followers widened. One of the first outsiders to join was 12-year-old Ann Putnam, daughter of Thomas Putnam, a local farmer whose family owned a lot of land and wielded much social influence in Salem. Next came Mary Walcott, whose father was a militia captain in the village. Sixteen-year-old Elizabeth Hubbard, the niece of the local doctor, William Griggs, also joined Tituba's circle, as did Susan Sheldon, Elizabeth Booth, Mercy Lewis, and Mary Warren, all in their late teens.

Each member of this covert group was sworn to secrecy. Clearly, none of them wished to be punished, which was sure to happen if their parents found out. However, the children did not appreciate an important fact of life and human nature, which is that the more people there are who know a secret, the more likely it is that the secret will be revealed. They were also unprepared for their hidden games to take a serious and frightening turn, which they did. One day when they dropped an egg white into some water, it formed a shape that to Tituba and the girls looked like a coffin, a symbol of death and ill fortune. This proved to be the fateful turning point for the girls and for their community. The girls then began to exhibit the convulsions and other disturbing physical behaviors that would lead to the witch trials.

Fear-Induced Lies

It is difficult to know specifically what drove Betty, Abigail, and the other girls to display these weird behaviors. Some of the girls may have interpreted the coffin-shaped egg white as a sign that they would have bleak futures. It is also possible that some or all of them viewed the death symbol as a sign from God, admonishing them for playing forbidden games. However, probably more of the girls' growing trepidation was caused by fear and guilt already programmed into them by the society in which they lived. On the one hand, there was guilt over having flirted with evil forces, which they believed could land them in hell. There was also surely a lurking fear that their elders would find out what they had been doing and subject them to terrible punishments, and possibly even expel them from the community.

Most modern scholars suspect that deep-rooted guilt about practicing magic and the fear of getting caught weighed heavily on the young women, especially on Abigail and the older girls. Certainly they, like other Puritan children, had been systematically and thoroughly programmed with a strong fear of evil, the devil, demons, witches, and so forth. Puritan children commonly and frequently heard lectures and sermons warning of the dire consequences for young people who broke the rules of family and society. The following passage from a children's book by Cotton Mather was typical of the time:

They which lie must go to their father, the devil, into everlasting burning: they which never pray, God will pour out his wrath upon them; and, when they beg and pray in hell-fire, God will not forgive them, but there they must lie forever.[14]

Abigail Williams and her playmates likely had already heard speeches such as this hundreds of times in their young lives: Nagging fear of eternal damnation was almost certainly an ever-present part of their worldview. Modern physicians and psychologists have shown that such fears can, in some people, manifest themselves in debilitating physical symptoms.

Whatever their personal motivations may have been, in January 1692, the girls in Tituba's circle began displaying such symptoms. It appears that Betty and Abigail were the first to be afflicted. Reverend and Mrs. Parris noticed the girls were cowering in corners, entering trancelike states, and uttering meaningless words and phrases. Worst of all, like Ann Cole in Hartford and the Goodwin children in Boston, Betty and Abigail started throwing fits. Deodat Lawson, a Puritan minister who visited Salem that winter, described the following incident at the Parris house:

Naming Names

A number of historians think that the power of suggestion likely played an integral part in the initial naming of witches by the afflicted girls of Salem Village. At first, the girls claimed they did not know who was harassing them. Only after their elders asked about specific people who were already disliked in the community did the girls agree that those named were witches. As Marion L. Starkey, a scholar of the Salem trials, wrote:

> The simple "Who torments you?" had been proved ineffectual. Leading questions were now put to the girls … Names of old suspects were now suggested to the girls and their reactions sharply studied. Parris for his part found his mind turning to Tituba. Now that he looked back, he recalled that Betty and Abigail had been with the untutored slave more often than was good for them … So the questions were put, and locked though the girls were in their own private world, in the hypnoid state to which they periodically achieved they could not indefinitely remain impervious to the power of such persistent suggestion.[1]

1. Marion L. Starkey, *The Devil in Massachusetts: A Modern Enquiry into the Salem Witch Trials*. New York, NY: Random House, 1989, pp. 47–48.

In the beginning of the evening I went to pay Mr. Parris a visit. When I was there, his kinswoman, Abigail Williams … had a grievous fit. She was at first harried with violence to and fro in the room …sometimes making as if she would fly, stretching up her arms as high as she could, and crying, "Whish, Whish, Whish!" several times. [She then claimed she saw an invisible witch in the room.] After that, she ran to the fire and began to throw firebrands about the house and [to] run … as if she would run up [the] chimney.[15]

Soon the rest of the girls in Tituba's circle were displaying the same symptoms, including violent fits. Meanwhile, one of the girls, Mary Walcott, appeared to have been bitten by some invisible entity, and Elizabeth Hubbard claimed she had been stalked by a pack of wolves, creatures widely associated with evil.

Pointing Fingers

The parents of the afflicted girls were, quite understandably, disturbed and concerned by these odd behaviors and incidents. Parris at first resorted to fasting and praying. He hoped that these traditional religious rituals would make the strange symptoms go away. When this approach did not work, Parris called on Dr. Griggs and other Puritan physicians. After a thorough examination, Griggs pronounced that Betty and Abigail must be "under an evil hand."[16] In other words, the devil, a witch, or some other evil being was causing their symptoms. This is not surprising. First, he and other doctors of his day knew almost nothing about psychological traumas and ailments. Also, he had the case of the Goodwin children as a precedent; their fits had been "proven" to be caused by evil beings, he reasoned, so the Parris girls' fits must have the same cause.

Meanwhile, the girls' fits became more frequent and dramatic. Interestingly, this happened only after people from outlying farms, as well as Salem Town, started congregating in the village, eager to witness the young women's afflictions. It was as if the girls enjoyed being the center of attention and gave the crowds more of what they came to see. They even began having convulsions in church on Sunday.

Women and girls were supposed to be quiet during church services, but the girls interrupted the services often. They did more than just have fits, too. They sometimes told the person delivering the sermon to sit down, and they would sometimes exclaim that the sermon was too long. These remarks against the church and its leaders were seen as signs of the devil's work. The girls also interrupted church services to claim that they were seeing visions, including a recurring vision of a bird in the church.

Extremely concerned, Mary Walcott's aunt, Mary Sibley, decided to try using a traditional English remedy to catch a witch. It involved baking a witch cake, which consisted of rye-flour mixed with the urine of the suspected victim of a witch and fed to a dog. There are various beliefs on how the witch cake worked, whether the witch would be drawn to the dog or the affliction transferred to the animal. However, Puritans at that time believed the remedy would point out the guilty witch.

Guided by Sibley, John Indian baked the witch cake, and they fed it to the Parris family's dog. (Dogs were commonly associated with witches at that time.) Reverend Parris later reprimanded Mary Sibley, saying that she had rashly used the devil's tools to combat the devil. He even forced her to apologize to the entire community in church.

The witch cake had failed to stop the fits and other disturbing behaviors of Salem Village's afflicted girls. However, the girls knew about the cake and were aware that it was designed in part to identify the witch or witches who were tormenting them. Perhaps that is why days after baking the witch

This rendering of a scene in court shows Mary Walcott having a conveniently timed fit to help with the persecution of one of the accused witches.

cake, Betty and Abigail first accused a specific person of being a witch. They claimed Tituba was the evil witch causing their pain. The very next day, Ann Putnam and other afflicted girls began naming names, too. They accused two older women in the village—Sarah Good and Sarah Osborne—of being witches. In this way, the hysterical behavior of a few misguided young women began to infect their community with unreasonable fear and ruined the reputations and lives of hundreds of innocent people.

Chapter Three

PUBLIC ACCUSATIONS LEAD TO QUESTIONING

Accusations began spreading among the members of Salem Village fairly quickly after the girls' first fits had occurred. It is no surprise that the three women the girls first accused—Tituba, Sarah Good, and Sarah Osborne—were among the lower members of society. Their low social standing and the fact that they were women in a patriarchal, or male-dominated, society, meant that they had no actual chance of clearing their name and banishing the rumors.

Days after the public accusations were made, formal complaints were brought to Salem Town to begin the process of charging the three women. The complaints came from four men of Salem, one of which was Ann Putnam's father. Later that same day, warrants were issued for the arrest of the three women, and they were immediately brought in for initial questioning. Two

magistrates, John Hathorne and Jonathan Corwin, issued the warrants and were responsible for questioning the three women. The questioning was set to take place at a tavern in Salem Village. All three women were believed to be guilty, so the magistrates concluded that there was enough evidence and cause to have a proper trial.

This initial questioning sparked the witch hunt that ultimately killed 20 people and ruined the lives of more than 200. Eventually, the hysteria reached such a dangerous height that people accused and prosecuted Dorothy Good, the four-year-old daughter of Sarah Good. Throughout those two months, trials were set, testimonies were given, and more lies were created to cover the previous ones. Since most of these suspected witches were never highly regarded by the citizens of Salem, a verdict that affirmed their innocence remained unreachable from the very beginning.

Individuality as a Sin

The initial accusations of witchcraft were heavily motivated by the fear, ignorance, cruelty, and lack of charity inherent in Puritan society. History has shown that such societies tend to suspect, shun, isolate, and persecute the weakest and least conformist of their own members. Certainly it is no coincidence that the first people accused of being witches were not wealthy citizens with glowing reputations and connections in high places. Nor is it surprising that, at first, no men were accused; after all, men were seen as the community's leading citizens and the guardians and enforcers of order and conformity.

Rather, the initial targets were older women whose reputations were already questionable. As women, they were assumed from the start to be weak, gullible, corruptible, and more susceptible than men to falling under the control of evil forces. Another strike against these women was that they were physically unattractive and aging. Puritan society disapproved of women whose faces were wrinkled, whose flesh was sagging, and whose bodies were stooped by years of back-breaking work. Still another reason to suspect the women was their outspokenness. People, particularly women, who complained too much, asked too many questions, or said or did things that the community deemed even slightly out of the ordinary were seen as troublemakers and potential agents of sin and evil. Such women, Carol F. Karlsen pointed out, "risked not only society's vengeance, but also the loss of approval and love of the people closest to them—most particularly their own fathers."[17] The fact that the women were poor and economically and politically powerless also made them easy targets.

Tituba, the first to be accused of practicing witchcraft, conveniently fit all of these criteria. Not only was she a woman, she was foreign-born, had dark skin, and spoke with a discernible accent. Moreover, Tituba hailed from a non-Christian society that had, by English and Puritan standards, strange, unwholesome customs, including some that were associated with magic and evil beings. Considering these attributes in a witch hunt in a white, Christian community, the woman from Barbados "was an inevitable suspect," as Marion L. Starkey wrote:

> If Salem Village contained anyone at all who deliberately practiced the black arts, it was she. That the girls did not indict her earlier ... can only have been due to a not unreasonable fear of what Tituba, under cross-examination, might say about them. Guilt is an indispensable ingredient in the witch's broth of hysteria.[18]

The second victim of the witch hysteria, Sarah Good, also bore, in addition to her gender, a number of social black marks that made her a likely suspect. First, she was poor and lived in disgrace on the fringes of the community. Her poverty had been the result of a series of financial disasters during her two marriages, which had left her a destitute beggar. Her standing as a disgraced member of society came in part from the suicide of her father, John Solart, in 1672, which was an act condemned by all Puritans. Sarah Good's physical appearance also made her a natural suspect in the witch hunt. Though she was only around 40 years old, her hard life had taken a toll, and she looked closer to 70, with a bent back, a wrinkled face, prematurely gray hair, and a raspy voice. In other words, she looked and sounded like the stereotype of a witch.

Sarah Osborne, the third woman the girls accused of being a witch, also had a difficult life. Her prosperous first husband, Robert Prince, had died, after which she had married her penniless indentured servant, Alexander Osborne. Later, she had become disabled; by the time she was accused of witchcraft, she was 49 years old, poverty-stricken, and bedridden from illness. Because of her physical infirmity, Sarah Osborne could not make it to church on Sundays. This was another black mark against her, as Puritan elders expected everyone to attend services, no matter how physically incapacitated they might be.

Guilty Until Proven Innocent

On the morning of March 1, 1692, as Sarah Osborne, Sarah Good, and Tituba were led to Nathaniel Ingersoll's tavern, the weather in the region of Salem was finally clearing after nearly a week of storms. Though many of the roads in the area were flooded and impassable, hundreds of people flocked from all around to witness the questioning. In fact, the crowd became so large that the tavern could not hold them all, so the magistrates in charge of the proceedings, Hathorne and Corwin, decided to move them to the nearby meetinghouse.

Although the questioning was a serious legal procedure, neither of these officials had any formal legal training. This was partly because, at the time, the only professional school in the colony—Harvard College—prepared young men for the ministry only. Also, there simply were no qualified lawyers in the Massachusetts Bay Colony. "The Puritans had a low opinion of lawyers," Starkey pointed out,

and did not permit the professional practice of law in the colony. In effect, the administration of the law was in the hands of laymen, most of them second-generation colonists who had an incomplete grasp of current principles of English jurisdiction.[19]

Under these circumstances, the

accused women were at still another disadvantage—they lacked legal rights and representation. The men in charge of both the questioning sessions and trials had little understanding of the old English idea that an accused person is innocent until proven guilty. Moreover, none of the public officials who ran these proceedings "saw any reason to provide an accused witch with right of counsel ... and their notions of evidence and of courtroom etiquette were, to put it mildly, peculiar."[20]

Thus, when Hathorne began the first round of questioning, singling out Sarah Good, he did not conduct himself as an impartial fact gatherer, as would have been the fair and proper approach. Instead, he acted like a zealous prosecutor who is certain the suspect is guilty and is eager to force a confession from her:

> "Sarah Good," Hathorne asked, "what evil spirit have you familiarity with?" She replied, "None." Working from prepared notes Hathorne continued as if she had said just the opposite. Had she contracted with the devil? Why did she hurt these children? What creature did she employ to do so? He proceeded less like a judge than a police interrogator; it fell to him to establish not the truth of the charges but the guilt of the suspect.[21]

In the moments that followed, the magistrate asked Betty and the other girls if they were sure that this woman, Sarah Good, was their tormentor. The girls insisted she was. Furthermore, they said, Good had harassed them that very morning by sending her specter, or invisible evil spirit, to pinch and assault them. Hathorne continued to interrogate Good: "Do you not see now what you have done? Why do you not tell us the truth? Why do you thus torment these poor children?"[22] Good remained steadfast in her claim that she was innocent. However, the magistrates, in their narrow-minded rush to judgment, decided she must be lying and therefore should be held for trial.

Sarah's Accusation

Sarah Osborne was next to be questioned. Hathorne asked her some of the same initial questions he had asked Sarah Good, beginning with what evil spirits she was familiar with. Osborne declared that she had no such familiarity, nor had she ever seen the devil, nor consorted with any of the devil's helpers. Then, Hathorne abruptly changed the direction of the questioning to her familiarity with Sarah Good. He was seeking to incriminate the present suspect by linking her with the other accused woman. Osborne denied having any familiarity with Sarah Good and claimed she had not seen her in two years. She went on to explain that the last encounter she had had with Sarah Good was one day when the two had seen each other on the road to Salem Town. They had merely exchanged brief hellos, Osborne claimed, and continued on their separate ways. "Sarah Good [said] that it

Harvard's Religious Roots

Although colonial Puritan society was extremely narrow-minded and strict—both religiously and socially—the Puritans placed a strong emphasis on education. They believed that men and women needed to be educated to a certain degree so that they could properly study the Bible. To that end, in 1635, members of the Massachusetts Bay Colony established the first public school in America—Boston Latin School. They also set up America's first college—Harvard College—in 1636. At first, the purpose of Harvard was to train local colonial ministers so that fewer churchmen would have to be imported from England. In time, however, the college offered courses in all the liberal arts, including mathematics and philosophy. It is perhaps ironic that the same society that demonstrated its ignorance by persecuting people for witchcraft created a school that became one of the most progressive, enlightened educational institutions in the world.

Harvard's primary function in the 1600s was to train ministers. Today, it is one of the most prestigious educational institutions in the world.

was you that hurt the children," Hathorne suddenly told Osborne. She retorted: "I do not know that the Devil goes about in my likeness to do any hurt."[23]

Next, as he had done earlier while questioning Sarah Good, Hathorne addressed himself to the afflicted girls. He asked them to confirm that Sarah Osborne had tormented them, and they replied in the affirmative. At this point, Osborne asserted that she was not only innocent, but also more likely to be the victim rather than the perpetrator of witchcraft. When Hathorne asked what she meant, she told him how she once had dreamed that she saw the form of a person with dark skin near her bed. It had pinched her and pulled her hair.

Finally, Hathorne attempted to further damage Osborne's image and reputation by emphasizing her lack of church attendance. She insisted that poor health had kept her from attending services. However, this did not satisfy Hathorne and Corwin. They decided that she, like Sarah Good, should be held for trial.

Tituba's Supernatural Affairs

The last woman to be questioned that day was Tituba. She had already been the subject of unusually great interest in the community because of her dark skin and foreign origins. However, after Sarah Osborne's testimony about having been tormented by a person with dark skin, the crowd was even more interested to hear what Tituba—who fit that description—had to say.

At first, she claimed that she had done the children no harm. However, her testimony later took a different turn, as she increasingly admitted her involvement in supernatural affairs. Exactly why she confessed to aiding in witchcraft is uncertain, but some experts suggest that she had been coached by Samuel Parris and Thomas Putnam, who wanted her to implicate Good and Osborne. Tituba told Hathorne and Corwin that there were women that would hurt the girls. When asked to name them, she answered Sarah Good, Sarah Osborne, and two other women who came to Salem from Boston accompanied by a strange tall man. In a long round of questioning, Tituba claimed that the four witches had been aided by several evil animals, including a black dog, a yellow bird, and some cats. All the witches and animals had sometimes taken invisible forms. Then, Hathorne concentrated on the tall man. "What clothes [does] the man appear [to] you in?" he inquired. "Black clothes sometimes,"[24] Tituba said. The implication, one that everyone in the room must have gathered, was that this tall man in black clothes was the devil himself.

Suddenly, Betty and Abigail began having convulsions, causing murmurs of astonishment and fear to ripple through the room. Hathorne quickly used this outburst to his advantage, asking Tituba, "Do you see who it is who torments these children now?"

"Yes," she replied. "It is Goody Good. She hurts them in her own shape."[25] ("Goody," which was short for "Goodwife," was a way to address women in Puritan society.) Then Tituba herself seemed to become speechless and threw a fit similar to that performed by the girls.

Tituba's testimony, whoever had coached it, proved pivotal because it did irreparable harm to Sarah Good and Sarah Osborne, as well as to the community.

First, the slave woman had confirmed community-wide suspicions and distrust of Good and Osborne. Also, Tituba had said that other witches were loose in the region, a revelation that significantly increased the witch-related hysteria that already existed in Salem. From that moment on, nearly everyone was on the lookout for evil witches in their midst.

As for the three women, for the time being, they were sent to a jail in Boston. The already ill and frail Sarah Osborne died there two months later, but Sarah Good was destined to stand trial for witchcraft. Meanwhile, because Tituba had confessed and told the magistrates what they wanted to hear, they did not need her to stand trial; they merely imprisoned her.

New Accusations

Early evidence that the wave of hysteria in Salem Village was growing came only a few days after Sarah Good, Sarah Osborne, and Tituba were carted off to prison. The afflicted girls continued to have seizure-like fits, but what was causing them now? In theory, if witchcraft was real, the specters of the imprisoned women could easily have floated from Boston to Salem and continued to harass the girls. Evidently this did not occur to Betty, Abigail, Ann, and the other children; in their minds, their accused tormentors were gone, so new suspects were needed to explain their continued fits and other symptoms.

Accordingly, on March 11, 1692, Ann Putnam claimed that she was being tormented by Martha Corey, an upstanding member of the community and a regular churchgoer. Thomas Putnam and some other men went to Corey's house on March 12 and questioned her informally. Then, on March 21, she was forced to appear for formal questioning at Ingersoll's tavern. According to the later report of the Reverend Deodat Lawson, three of the supposedly bewitched girls "vehemently accused [Corey] in the assembly of afflicting them, by biting, pinching, strangling, etc. and that they did in their fit see her likeness [i.e., her specter] coming to them."[26] In spite of Corey's repeated protestations of innocence, the magistrates were satisfied that she must be a witch and ordered her thrown into jail to await trial.

The accusations of witchcraft did not end with Martha Corey. On March 19, Abigail Williams claimed that the specter of another respectable churchgoer, Rebecca Nurse, was

Though Martha Corey was an upstanding member of the Salem Puritan community, after she was accused of being a witch, she was found guilty and placed in jail.

tormenting her. Some of the other afflicted girls soon confirmed that Nurse was a witch. On March 24, the 71-year-old woman was arrested and brought to the village meetinghouse for questioning. The proceedings turned into a raucous spectacle as the girls staged numerous fits, each time claiming that Rebecca Nurse's specter was assaulting them. Not surprisingly, she, too, was sent off to jail.

That same day, Dorothy Good, the four-year-old daughter of Sarah Good, was put on display in the

One Dog, Two Cats, and a Yellow Bird

During magistrate John Hathorne's questioning of Tituba on March 1, 1692, she described how the devil and his followers took the forms of a number of animals:

> The court asked about other specters, so she told them the spirits appeared "sometimes like a hog, sometimes like a great black dog."
>
> "But what did they say unto you?"
>
> "The black dog said, 'Serve me.' But I said, 'I am afraid.' He said if I did not, he would do worse to me."
>
> "What did you say to it?"
>
> "'I will serve you no longer.' Then he said he would hurt me. And then he looks like a man and threatens to hurt me."
>
> "What other creatures have you seen?"
>
> Question followed answer as she described the yellow bird, one of the "pretty things" the man offered as bribes, and the aggressive cats "one red, another black as big as a little dog."[1]

1. Quoted in Marilynne K. Roach, *The Salem Witch Trials: A Day-by-Day Chronicle of a Community Under Siege*, New York, NY: Taylor Trade, 2002, p. 29.

meetinghouse after being named as a witch; the defenseless child, who had no real idea of what was happening, soon ended up in prison with the other accused witches.

Some residents of Salem now felt that the witch hunt had gone too far. They showed the courage to doubt the claims made by the afflicted girls and immediately paid a heavy price for it. One of these brave individuals was farmer John Proctor, whose servant was Mary Warren, one of the girls having fits. When he said that all the girls deserved a good thrashing and indicated that he might whip the truth out of Mary, the girls promptly accused his wife, Elizabeth, of being a witch. John Proctor strenuously objected and, as a result, was himself accused of witchcraft and arrested.

Similarly, when Sarah Cloyce

Notifying the Suspects

The magistrates in Salem Town issued numerous arrest warrants during the roundup of suspected witches from late February through May 1692. Most of these warrants featured text that was identical or similar to this one for the arrest of Rebecca Nurse, dated March 23, 1692:

There being complaint this day made before us, by Edward Putnam and Jonathan Putnam … both of Salem Village, against Rebecca Nurse, the wife of Frances Nurse of Salem Village, for vehement suspicion of having committed [diverse] acts of witchcraft and thereby having done much hurt and injury to the bodies of Ann Putnam … the daughter of said Thomas Putnam, and Abigail Williams … You are therefore in their Majesties' names hereby required to apprehend and bring before us Rebecca Nurse … tomorrow about eight of the clock in the aforenoon, at the house of [Lieutenant] Nathaniel Ingersoll in Salem Village, in order to her examination relating to the abovesaid premises, and hereof you are not to fail.[1]

1. Quoted in Paul Boyer and Stephen Nissenbaum, eds., *Salem-Village Witchcraft: A Documentary Record of Local Conflict in Colonial New England*, Boston, MA: Northeastern University Press, 1972, p. 22.

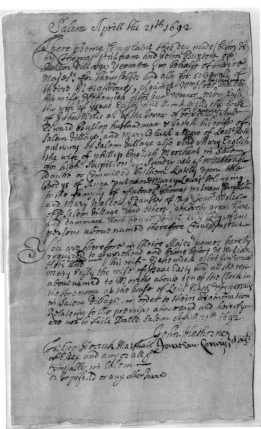

This arrest warrant for Sarah Wildes shows an example of what most warrants looked like at that time. Sarah Wildes was executed on July 19, 1692.

An Attempt at the Truth

Part of Hathorne's questioning of Rebecca Nurse, which occurred on March 24, 1692, went this way:

"Tell us," said the court when the racket subsided, "have you not had invisible appearances more than what is common in nature?"

"I have none, nor never had [any] in my life."

"Do you think these [afflicted girls] suffer voluntarily or involuntarily?" the magistrate asked, for some (Proctor, for example) doubted the genuineness of the "fits."

"I cannot tell."

"That is strange. Everyone can judge," he said (although Martha Corey's guesses had not impressed him).

"I must be silent."

"They accuse you of hurting them, and if you think it is not unwillingly but by design [that they are faking their fits], you must look upon them as murderers," he explained, for witchcraft was a hanging crime.

"I cannot tell what to think of it ..."

"Do you think these [girls] suffer against their wills or not?"

"I do not think [they] suffer against their wills."[1]

1. Quoted in Marilynne K. Roach, *The Salem Witch Trials: A Day-by-Day Chronicle of a Community Under Siege.* New York, NY: Taylor Trade, 2002, p. 54.

Rebecca Nurse's homestead remains intact to this day. It was restored in 1908 by the Rebecca Nurse Memorial Association.

defended her sister Rebecca Nurse, she was also accused and arrested. The circle of accusations and arrests was widening at an alarming rate and there seemed no end in sight. A remark John Proctor had made shortly before his arrest now seemed to ring true with a vengeance. If the afflicted girls were allowed to continue making their fantastic accusations, he had said, "we should all be [labeled] devils and witches quickly."[27] Proctor's words foreshadowed his own fate and the fate of many others in Salem. The hysteria showed no signs of going away.

Chapter Four

THE WITCHES' FATE

The formal trials began in June of 1692. By this point, several other individuals had been accused of witchcraft and were in jail awaiting the start of the trials. This number, believed to be about 70 at first, only increased throughout the progression of the trials. Several towns outside of Salem began accusing people of witchcraft as well. The uproar of the accusations began to spread quickly and rapidly, leaving the fear that no one was safe from their name being tied to accusations of witchcraft. In turn, mass hysteria began to settle in among people throughout Eastern Massachusetts. This fear stemmed from many different factors, and it continued to grow, ruining the lives of everyone caught in its path.

One of the biggest factors in this continued hysteria was the girls who began the accusations. After all the uproar that surrounded the accused witches began to spread, the afflicted girls could not possibly retract their accusations. Even as young girls, the understanding of the magnitude of punishment linked with that kind of lie was too much to bear. Similarly, the elders that stood with the young girls did not want to their credibility to be ruined, which in turn, would ruin their reputation. The answer was to continue the trials, each person going into them with a personal mission to not come out as a liar. This fact alone caused the intense persistence that lead to the loss of so many lives.

Attempts were made to find the actual truth among the afflicted girls. Mary Warren, one of the accusers, was threatened with a beating to get her to confess to her manipulations and lies. After this threat, Warren's fits magically stopped, and she claimed to

This is the front of the courthouse where all of the suspected witches' trials were held.

no longer be afflicted by the forces of the devil. This led to a switch in stories from the other afflicted girls. In fear that they would be pegged as liars, they turned on Warren, and they stated that she herself switched teams and began working with the devil and practicing witchcraft. After an intensive session of questioning, Warren retracted her previous statement of no longer being afflicted and continued on with the other girls. It is obvious that Mary Warren realized her only chance of survival was to continue lying and to go along with whatever the other girls suggested.

Following this incident, the trials continued. What then occurred was the effect of sheer fear among an entire community, based on the accusations of a few young girls. The unfortunate events that progressed next resulted in the execution of several members of the community who were found guilty by all means, only later to have it all shrugged off as a misunderstanding.

Evidence

The trials could not begin until the Massachusetts Bay Colony had a new charter from England. The colony's original charter had lapsed three years before, leaving its inhabitants in a sort of legal limbo in which no legally sanctioned trials could be conducted. To remedy this situation, the widely respected minister Increase Mather had recently journeyed to England to petition the government for a new colonial charter. He returned in mid-May 1692 with the charter in hand, which meant that the trials could begin shortly afterward.

Mather brought with him a new colonial governor, William Phips, whose authority was needed to set up the court and appoint its judges. Phips arrived to see the local jails overflowing and realized that he had his work cut out for him. In a letter addressed to his superiors in England, he wrote:

When I first arrived I found this province miserably harassed with a most Horrible witchcraft or Possession of Devils, which had broke in upon several Towns, some scores of poor people were taken with preternatural torments ... There were many committed to the prison upon suspicion of witchcraft before my arrival. The loud cries and clamors of the friends of the afflicted people ... and many others prevailed with me to give a Commission of Oyer and Terminer for discovering what witchcraft might be at the bottom [of this turmoil].[28]

The "Oyer and Terminer" Phips mentioned was an old Anglo-French legal phrase that meant "to hear and determine." It referred to a special court convened to hear criminal cases. Phips authorized the creation of the court in early June and selected seven judges. One was the deputy (or

A Formal Explanation

In a letter sent in October 1692 to his superiors in England, William Phips, the new governor of the Massachusetts Bay Colony, tried his best to describe the strange situation in which a number of local girls had seizures that seemed to be caused by supernatural forces. Phips said in part,

> The court still proceeded in the same method of trying [the witches], which was by the evidence of the afflicted persons, who when they were brought into the court ... instantly fell to the ground in strange agonies and grievous torments, but when touched by them upon the arm or some other part of their flesh they immediately revived and came to themselves ... When I inquired into the matter, I was informed by the Judges that they begin with this [evidence of the fits], but [also] had human testimony against such [persons] as were condemned and undoubted proof of their being witches. But at length I found that the Devil did take upon him the shape of Innocent persons.[1]

1. Quoted in Frances Hill, ed., *The Salem Witch Trials Reader*. New York, NY: Da Capo, 2000, p. 102.

lieutenant) governor, William Stoughton, who resided in Dorchester. The others were Bostonians John Richards, Peter Sergeant, Samuel Sewall, and Waitstill Winthrop, along with Nathaniel Saltonstall from Haverhill and Bartholomew Gedney from Salem.

In a later letter home, Phips stated: "I depended on the court for a right method of proceeding in cases of witchcraft."[29] By "method," Phips meant the kinds of evidence that would be admissible in the witchcraft trials. At the time, based on precedent in earlier cases in the colony and in England, several kinds of evidence were allowed that today would be viewed as highly prejudiced, even nonsensical. For example, one kind of evidence that supposedly proved someone was an agent of the devil was his or her inability to recite the Lord's Prayer without error. Also, if someone who had confessed to being a witch (as Tituba had) proceeded to accuse someone else of the same, it was seen as acceptable evidence. There was also spectral evidence—claims made by various persons that they had witnessed invisible specters harassing people. (Oddly, few seemed to question the fact that some people could see these apparitions, while others could not.)

During a touch test, the accused was forced to touch someone who was having a witchcraft-induced fit. If the fit suddenly stopped, it supposedly proved that the specter afflicting the victim had jumped back into the body of the accused, and therefore, the accused was guilty.

Other kinds of acceptable evidence in witchcraft cases involved the discovery of physical proof on the bodies of the accused. As part of the trial, a defendant was taken into a room and closely examined. If any mark was found on his or her skin, it was believed to be the mark of the devil. These marks could be flat or bumpy, could be red or brown, and could even be oddly shaped. A pin test was then performed, in which the examiner pierced the mark with a pin. If it did not bleed, it was viewed as another sign of the devil's work.

The First Case

As it turned out, a very different use of pins became evidence of witchcraft in the initial case tried by the court of Oyer and Terminer when it convened on June 2. Now commonly called voodoo dolls, miniature images pierced with pins had long been standard instruments of black magic in Europe and elsewhere. Supposedly, a puppet represented an enemy, and

when the puppet was pricked with a pin, that enemy suffered harm. These dolls and the pins stuck in them were used as proof that Bridget Bishop, a tavern keeper in her late 50s or early 60s, was practicing witchcraft.

Bishop was the first person to be tried as a witch in Salem. From the paranoid point of view of Puritan society, Bishop had a number of black marks against her that had made her an inevitable suspect in the witch hysteria. About 12 years before, she had been accused of evil doings, though she had never been legally tried. Rumors spread that she had bewitched some horses and turned herself into a cat.

There was also damning testimony from a number of Bishop's neighbors and acquaintances, who recounted strange events that happened when she was around. One modern expert on the trials summarized the testimony of William Stacey, the son of a Salem mill operator:

> Coins disappeared from his pocket after she paid him for work. His cart became stuck in a hole right after he told her how some folk suspected she was a witch, only there was no hole. He then talked ... about the time her specter invaded his room ... Stacey testified about her stealing his father's brass [a metal object from the family mill], he got tossed against a stone wall and down a bank one night. After that, his cart collapsed entirely the next time

Bridget Bishop was hanged on Gallows Hill on June 10, 1692.

he passed her. But worse yet, his daughter Priscilla, a healthy child, fell ill and died within two weeks.[30]

Stacey's testimony was typical of the witch hysteria and trials of the period. It was quite common to blame ordinary accidents and unfortunate events, including naturally occurring deaths, on suspected witches.

Though the testimony given against Bishop by Stacey and other neighbors was damaging, the court was most swayed by the so-called evidence found by workmen who had helped to renovate a house Bishop had lived in a few years before. They claimed they had torn "down the cellar wall of the old house," and "in holes in the old wall" they had "found several puppets made up of rags and hogs' bristles with headless pins in them with the points outward."[31]

When asked about the puppets hidden in the wall, Bridget Bishop claimed she had no idea how they got there. However, the judges and men making up the jury did not believe her, partly because they already assumed she must be guilty. As in all the cases heard in the Salem witch trials, the initial questionings determined the suspects' guilt. The court trials constituted little more than legal confirmation of guilt. Thus, no one was surprised when the court found Bishop guilty of being a witch and sentenced her to be executed.

Punishment

Another aspect of the Salem witch trials that differs from modern legal proceedings is that those found guilty had no recourse to legal appeals and received no mercy of any kind. Today in the United States, because of an extended series of appeals, an execution takes place several years after the convicted person is sentenced. In 17th-century Salem, justice, if it can be called that, was much swifter. On June 10, 1692, only eight days after her trial, Bridget Bishop was taken to Gallows Hill (later called Witches' Hill), located not far southwest of Salem Town.

The other 18 victims who later received the same sentence were doomed to undergo essentially the same procedure that Bishop did that morning. First, her hands were bound tightly, and she was placed in a wooden cart. A constable drove the cart down the town's main street while guards rode alongside to keep the onlookers at bay. There were hundreds of these spectators, who had come from all the neighboring towns to take a ghoulish sort of delight in seeing someone suffer and die. Most members of the crowd cruelly shouted at and mocked the prisoner as the cart made its way to the hill of death. One local man, Jonathan Cary, who pitied the condemned individuals, later wrote a letter to the magistrates complaining about the vicious and heartless conduct of the spectators. "To speak of their usage of the prisoners," he said, "and the inhumanity shown to them of the time of their execution, no sober Christian could bear. They had also [in addition to their court trials] trials of cruel mockings."[32]

When the cart, still surrounded by jeering people, reached Gallows Hill, Bridget Bishop was removed and escorted up the side of the hill. At the summit, a ladder had been set up beneath a stout branch of a large oak tree, from which a noosed rope hung. Bridget Bishop's sentence of death by public hanging was then carried out by an executioner.

In this pitiless way, Bridget Bishop died. The extreme cruelty shown to her in life continued in the minutes following her demise. The executioner cut her down, and the guards tossed her body into a makeshift grave (in some accounts a rocky crevice) in the side of the hill. No prayers were said, no marker was placed on the grave, and no one was allowed to stay and pay their respects.

Skepticism Among the Judges

The trial and execution of Bridget Bishop sent a shudder through the Puritan communities of Massachusetts. Certainly the other accused witches in jail now despaired more than ever for their own lives. If Bishop had been found guilty and hanged so quickly, would they suffer similarly? Also, a few people in high places were disturbed for different reasons. One

of the judges, Nathaniel Saltonstall, thought that the evidence against Bishop had been flimsy. Moreover, he felt that the way she was treated on the day of her execution was un-Christian and reprehensible, so he resigned from the court. Jonathan Corwin, who had helped run the pre-trial questioning sessions, took his place. In addition, a group of local ministers voiced their concerns about the admission of spectral evidence in the trials. Like Saltonstall, they worried that it was unreliable. However, the remaining judges disagreed, and such evidence remained admissible.

The witch trials resumed on June 28. On that day and the two that followed, five women were tried: Sarah Good, Sarah Wildes, Elizabeth Howe, Susannah Martin, and Rebecca Nurse. As had happened during the earlier questioning sessions, Betty Parris, Abigail Williams, and the other supposedly afflicted girls were allowed to be present. The girls repeatedly threw fits and claimed that the defendants' specters were tormenting them.

Sarah Good became the second person found guilty in the trials, and she went to her death on Gallows Hill on July 19. Right to the end, a local minister, Nicholas Noyes, harassed her and called her a witch. At the last moment, Good stunned the crowd by loudly telling him, "You are a liar … I am no more a witch than you are a wizard, and if you take away my life God will give you blood to drink."[33] According

This image from the early 1900s shows Gallows Hill, where several innocent victims were hanged during the Salem witch trials.

A Change in Verdict

One of the jurors in Rebecca Nurse's trial, Thomas Fisk, later explained why the jury had first found her innocent, then changed the verdict to guilty:

> July 4, 1692. I Thomas Fisk … being one of them that were of the Jury the last week at Salem-Court, upon the [Trial] of [Rebecca] Nurse, etc., being desired by some of the Relations why the Jury brought her in Guilty after her Verdict [of] not Guilty; I do hereby give my reasons to be as follows … When the Verdict [of] not Guilty was [given], the [honored] Court was pleased to object against it … After the honored [judges of the] Court had [reminded the jurors about some phrases Nurse had uttered in the past], several of the Jury declared themselves desirous to go out again, and thereupon the [honored] Court gave leave … [These phrases, which] were affirmed to have been spoken by her … were to me [the] principal Evidence against her.[1]

1. Quoted in "The Trial of Rebecca Nurse," Famous American Trials, Salem Witchcraft Trials, 1692. www.law.umkc.edu/faculty/projects/ftrials/salem/ASA_NUR.HTM.

to tradition, this was eventually fulfilled. Some local records claim that 25 years later, Noyes choked to death on blood from internal bleeding.

In the eyes of those present, the most remarkable of the five cases tried at the end of June 1692 was that of Rebecca Nurse. Thirty-nine local residents mustered the nerve to sign a petition in her behalf. One of them was the influential John Putnam (brother of Thomas Putnam), who had earlier denounced Nurse but then changed his mind. The document stated in part: "We never had any cause or grounds to suspect her of any such thing as she is now accused of."[34] The members of the jury found themselves agreeing with the petitioners, as Nurse presented herself in court as a respectable Christian woman. Thus, the jury initially found her innocent.

However, this verdict was not destined to stand, because too many people had either a vested interest in or a strong expectation of finding all five women guilty. Immediately after the verdict was announced, the afflicted girls went into violent spasms. At the same time, hundreds of onlookers, including those who had earlier denounced and questioned the defendants, cried out in loud voices. Meanwhile, outside the building, the news of the verdict caused dozens of people to have fits almost as bad as those of the girls inside.

Seeing all this commotion, the surprised and terrified judges concluded that the jury must have made a mistake. They admonished the jurors to reconsider, and Rebecca Nurse's verdict was changed to guilty. At the last moment, Governor Phips granted her a reprieve. However, another hysterical public outcry scared him into recalling it, and Nurse was hanged on July 19, along with Good, Wildes, Howe, and Martin. Hearing of their convictions and deaths, the other prisoners became distraught. It had begun to look as though everyone who had been accused of witchcraft would soon meet similar fates.

Chapter Five

TUNNEL VISION

After the first several deaths of the trials, the court continued to persecute and question citizens for witchcraft. By this point, the magnitude of the situation still had not begun to weigh on the townspeople. Hundreds of people were jailed, and many were hanged. At the peak of the hysteria, community members still were not able to see the ridiculous nature of their accusations. The idea of witches tormenting local men and women consumed the village of Salem, and as the trials progressed, the insane notion that the devil was among them only intensified. The courts relied heavily on torture and hearsay to conduct these trials and to attempt to get confessions out of the accused witches. The tunnel vision of all the people of power in the community led to inaccurate representations of the cases in question, which in turn, made it impossible to see the foolishness of the accusations.

Petitions were filed, and complaints were made among the people of Salem. However, no retrials were granted, and under most circumstances, if a person was accused, they were most likely convicted and found guilty. Several accused were hanged, and hundreds remained in jail with their lives but were responsible for paying for their food and keep. This generally resulted in the loss of land and all property, leaving them destitute and helpless upon release.

Reconsideration

One appeal had been lodged by Rebecca Nurse shortly before her execution. After her jury had been coerced to reconsider its verdict of innocence, she had been recalled to the courtroom to clarify some earlier testimony.

Shown here is an artist's idea of what it might have looked like when a woman accused of being a witch was arrested.

One of the points that needed clarification was her statement that Deliverance Hobbs was "one of us." This statement was important to jurors because Hobbs was an accused witch. Some believed Nurse's words placed her in league with Hobbs and the other supposed witches.

When Nurse was brought back to court, a juror asked her a question about her statement concerning Hobbs. However, because Nurse was partly deaf, as well as elderly, ill, and distraught, she did not hear it and remained silent. Only later was she told that she had been asked the question and had failed to answer it, thereby sealing her fate. She therefore wrote an appeal to the court, explaining that she had simply not heard the question. Nurse also explained that her statement about Hobbs reflected their shared status as prisoners, not as witches. However, the judges, like almost everyone else in Salem, were too swept up in the wave of public hysteria to give this appeal fair treatment.

Four days after Nurse was hanged on Gallows Hill, John Proctor, still in his jail cell, penned a longer, more moving plea. It was addressed to Increase Mather and four other prominent local ministers. Evidently, Proctor hoped that these supposedly learned and godly men would somehow transcend the existing paranoid atmosphere and use their influence to stop the trials. "Nothing but our innocent blood will serve" those who had accused him and his cellmates of witchcraft, he wrote. The judges had unfairly "condemned us already before our trials," Proctor complained. Therefore, he and his fellow inmates "beg and implore your favorable assistance of this our humble petition ... that if it be possible our innocent blood may be spared."[35]

In the same letter, Proctor exposed another grossly unjust and brutal tactic employed by the authorities in their zeal to root out and destroy suspected witches. He pointed out that much of the so-called evidence against him and the others had been provided by five other suspected witches who had given said evidence under duress. In particular, at least two of these individuals had been tortured. They "would not confess anything," Proctor said, "till they tied them neck and heels till the blood was ready to come out of their noses."[36] The "neck and heels" torture consisted of looping a rope around a person's neck and then tying it to his or her ankles; this caused extreme discomfort, pain, and often nosebleeds.

Unfortunately for Proctor, his petition for justice and fair treatment fell mostly on deaf ears. The same was true of a petition submitted to the authorities on behalf of Elizabeth Proctor and her husband by 32 of their friends and neighbors. It read in part: "God may permit Satan to impersonate, dissemble, and thereby abuse innocents ... As to what we have ever seen of [Elizabeth and John Proctor], upon our consciences we judge them innocent of the crime objected."[37]

The petitioners had brought up a point that had been debated by many in the colony in recent weeks. They held that the devil, with his evil cunning, could make an innocent person look guilty. In contrast, many other Puritans believed that only guilty people succumbed to the wiles of the devil; therefore, Elizabeth and John Proctor must be guilty.

An Attempt at Reason

It was this second view that prevailed when the Proctors went to trial on August 5, 1692. In fact, the proceedings went swiftly and, in essence, did no more than confirm the findings of the Proctors' memorable questioning session on April 11. As in all the hearings and trials, much of the testimony and evidence against the defendants had come from the afflicted girls, who were ever-present in the room. In addition, Tituba's husband, John Indian, had been present that day. He had initiated a commotion that had quickly turned into an uproar. Right after Mrs. Proctor took the stand, he shouted, "There is the woman who came in her shift and choked me."[38] Hearing that, the girls began moaning and twitching. Some of them claimed that Elizabeth Proctor's specter was, at that moment, crouched on one of the courtroom's ceiling beams.

That revelation caused a wave of fear to sweep over the spectators in the chamber.

Amid the girls' groans and cries and the mounting clamor coming from the onlookers in the room, the Proctors tried to inject the proverbial voice of reason into the proceedings. Elizabeth Proctor charitably attempted to calm Abigail Williams, who had just denounced her. Meanwhile, John Proctor ran to his wife's side as if to defend her. Seeing him, Abigail shouted, "Why, he can pinch as well as she!"[39] The implication was that the man's specter had begun to harass the girls, which sent the spectators into a tumult.

When the judges finally managed to restore order, it was already too late for the Proctors. The damage had been done, and any hopes they had that they would be able to use reason and common sense to reverse the course of the witchcraft hysteria had been dashed. One of the prosecutors lashed out at John Proctor, saying: "You see, the devil will deceive you! The children could see what you were going to do before [you did it]. I would advise you to repent, for the devil is bringing you out [exposing you]."[40]

Proctor, an assertive individual, must have been deeply disturbed that the court would take the word of some hysterical, untrustworthy children over his. However, the reality of the trials was that the magistrates and judges had been thoroughly drawn into the world the girls had manufactured. As Starkey wrote:

The common sense of these men had abdicated before the crazed fantasies of wenches in their teens ... Procter's reasoning was like blasphemy to the magistrates. With them, the devil had indeed taken over. This was his hour and [also the hour of] the power of darkness ... It was a logic that admitted only one reality, the affliction of these girls and their testimony as to its cause.[41]

Thus, when the Proctors entered the courtroom on August 5, the two were already guilty in the judges' eyes. The judges pronounced the expected ver-dict and sentenced the two to death. However, Elizabeth Proctor was pregnant at the time, so she was given a temporary reprieve until her baby was born, after which she was to be hanged. John Proctor went to his death on Gallows Hill on August 19. Either shortly before or after his untimely demise, the local authorities seized all his property and belongings. One of the magistrates seized his cattle, sold some at half their market value, and slaughtered the rest for sale to the West Indies. The house and barn were stripped of everything, even storage barrels and pots and pans.

Taking Everything

Roughly a decade after the conclusion of the Salem witch trials, a Boston merchant named Robert Calef published a synopsis of the trials titled *More Wonders of the Invisible World*. In this passage, he wrote about the seizure of John Proctor's property by the authorities:

> John Proctor and his wife being in prison, the sheriff came to his house and seized all the goods, provisions, and cattle that he could come at [find], and sold some of the cattle at half price, and killed others, and put them up [for sale in] the West-Indies; [they] threw out the beer out of a barrel, and carried away the barrel; emptied a pot of broth, and took away the pot, and left nothing in the house for the support of the children. No part of the said goods are known to be returned.[1]

1. Quoted in Edmund Clarence Stedman and Ellen Mackay Hutchinson, eds., *A Library of American Literature: From the Earliest Settlement to the Present Time: Later Colonial Literature*, New York, NY: Charles L. Webster & Company, 1891, p. 179.

Witnesses Full of Lies

The Proctors were not the only people tried in early August 1692. Martha Carrier, a resident of the town of Andover, and George Jacobs Sr., a 72-year-old grandfather who needed two canes to walk, also faced the judges and jury. Much of the evidence against Carrier was provided by neighbors who had had property disputes with her. Typical was the testimony of Benjamin and Sarah Abbot. They claimed they had argued with Martha Carrier about the proper placement of a boundary running between their two farms and that Carrier had lost her temper and threatened to get back at Benjamin Abbot. In his testimony, Abbot listed the afflictions supposedly caused by Carrier in her efforts to seek revenge:

> *Presently after [the dispute] I was taken with a swelling in my foot and then was taken with a pain in my side ... which led to a sore which was lanced by Dr. Prescott ... and put me to very great misery, so that it brought me almost to death's door and continued until Goodwife Carrier was taken ... by the constable, and that very day I began to grow better ... Ever since, [I] have [had] great cause to think that the [Goodwife] Carrier had a great hand in my sickness and misery [by practicing witchcraft].* [42]

In addition to supposed evidence of this nature, Martha Carrier was condemned on the accusations of several people who confirmed that she was a witch. These included her own sons, who were severely tortured in jail to force them to denounce their mother. Amid the presentation of all this trumped-up evidence, Carrier remained defiant, calling the witnesses and afflicted girls liars and the whole proceedings shameful. This annoyed and, in some cases, enraged the community's authority figures, including Cotton Mather, who later called her "the rampant hag" and "Queen of Hell." [43]

As for George Jacobs, one of the afflicted girls, Sarah Churchill, and a local boy, John DeRich, claimed that the old man's specter had chased or beaten them. Jacobs realized that he had no way of refuting such fantastic accusations and seemed resigned to his fate. He is credited with telling the magistrates, "Well, burn me or hang me. I will stand in the truth of [Jesus] Christ!" [44] The judges proceeded to oblige him by sentencing him to death. Jacobs and Martha Carrier were both hanged on August 19 with John Proctor. Afterward, the authorities went to Jacobs's home and confiscated everything, including his wife's wedding ring.

Strength from the Devil

Another person who lost his life on Gallows Hill on August 19 was the Reverend George Burroughs. His case demonstrated that the witchcraft hysteria in the colony had grown to such

The trial of George Jacobs, which is shown here, concluded with the authorities seizing all of his assets and leaving his wife in poverty.

proportions that even Puritan ministers were not safe. His trial was seen as particularly important because several people had accused him of being the evil leader of all the witches that had been afflicting the colony. Thus, a number of prominent members of the community attended Burroughs's trial, including noted ministers Increase Mather, Deodat Lawson, and John Hale.

The testimony against Burroughs was vivid. Because he was an

No Mercy for
Reverend George Burroughs

Among the many incriminating statements made against the Reverend George Burroughs during his trial was that of the afflicted girl Mercy Lewis:

On the 7th of May 1692, at evening I saw the apparition of Mr. George Burroughs whom I very well knew, which did grievously torture me and urged me to write in his

[evil devil's] book ... He told me that he ... had bewitched Mr. Shepherd's daughter, and that ... the devil was his servant ... Then he again tortured me most dreadfully and threatened to kill me, for he said that I should not [bear] witness against him. Also, he told me that he had made Abigail Hobbs a witch and several more [young women witches]. Then again he did most dreadfully torture me.[1]

1. Quoted in Frances Hill, ed., *The Salem Witch Trials Reader*. New York, NY: Da Capo, 2000, p. 197.

Though on the surface it seemed as if people in positions of religious power were safe, Reverend George Burroughs, shown here, was found guilty of witchcraft and hanged.

unusually muscular and strong man, witnesses claimed that his strength must have come from the devil. He was also accused of biting numerous people while in spectral form. One of the afflicted girls, Ann Putnam, gave a deposition that stated in part:

> On the 20th of April, 1692, at evening [I] saw the apparition [specter] of a minister at which [I] was grievously affrighted and cried out … [I asked] "Whence came you, and what is your name, for I will complain of you … if you be a wizard." And immediately I was tortured by him, being racked [stretched] and almost choked by him, and he tempted me to write in his [evil devil's] book, which I refused with loud outcries … Then presently he told me that his name was George Burroughs and that he had had three wives and that he had bewitched the first two of them to death.[45]

During the trial, which lasted only a couple of hours at most, Burroughs seemed rattled, despondent, even lost in thought. Perhaps he was in a state of shock over being accused of such awful crimes. He knew full well that he was innocent. Also, it is possible that he was wondering why God would allow him, a devoted minister, to suffer such lies and cruel treatment. Whatever the reason for Burroughs's silence on the stand, it made him seem all the more guilty to the judges, jury, and onlookers. No one was surprised when he was found guilty and sentenced to be hanged.

To Burroughs's credit, his presence of mind returned to him as he approached the hanging tree. A few seconds after he climbed the ladder beneath the noose, he turned to the assembled crowd and loudly proclaimed his innocence. Then, he did a brilliant thing by reciting the Lord's Prayer in moving tones and without making a single mistake. Puritan society and law held that a witch or other evil being was incapable of doing this, so a hush suddenly fell over the crowd; many people who a few moments before had taunted and jeered the minister now found themselves doubting his guilt. Seeing this unexpected turn of events, the authorities speedily hung Burroughs before he could rally any more support. They then buried him so hastily that, according to some accounts, his chin and hand remained sticking out from the ground.

Torture Turned to Murder

Not all the people tried for witchcraft and sentenced to die were executed by hanging, as Burroughs, Carrier, Jacobs, and Proctor were in August. In September, Giles Corey, a farmer in his 80s, suffered a considerably slower demise. Corey had testified against his own wife, Martha, in March, in large part because he did not grasp the gravity of the situation at the time. Later, in April, several

This stone bench can be found at the Salem Witch Trials Memorial, which commemorates the victims of the trials.

of the afflicted girls accused the old man himself, saying that his specter had tormented them. When questioned, Corey had insisted: "I never did hurt them."[46]

Evidently, Corey remained incredulous that he would actually be brought to trial for witchcraft. However, when he realized that his trial was indeed imminent, he began to worry what would happen to his property if he was convicted. Ignorant of the law, he decided that his best strategy was to clam up and say nothing further. Corey even refused to plead either guilty or not guilty before the court.

The authorities had very seldom encountered such stubbornness by someone accused of a crime. They tried to get Corey to enter a plea by submitting him to a torture called peine forte et dure (French for "a punishment hard and severe"), which was an old European method of obtaining confessions. It was also called pressing, because it consisted of making the victim lie face-up on the ground, placing a board on his or her chest, and then loading large rocks onto the board.

When Corey refused to speak, the authorities took him to a field near the courthouse and began pressing him

Denying Claims

Part of the questioning session of Giles Corey on April 19, 1692, is excerpted here:

[Corey:] I never did hurt them [the afflicted girls].

[Magistrate:] It is your appearance [that] hurts them, they charge you. Tell us what you have done.

[Corey:] I have done nothing to damage them.

[Magistrate:] Have you never entered into contract with the devil?

[Corey:] I never did.

[Magistrate:] What temptations have you had?

[Corey:] I never had temptations in my life …

[Magistrate:] What was it [that] frightened you in the barn?

[Corey:] I know nothing that frightened me there.

[Magistrate:] Why, here are three witnesses that heard you say so today.

[Corey:] I do not remember it.[1]

1. Quoted in Marilynne K. Roach, *The Salem Witch Trials: A Day-by-Day Chronicle of a Community Under Siege.* New York, NY: Taylor Trade, 2002, pp. 77–78.

while a crowd of onlookers watched.

They hoped that, at some point, the pressing would convince him to give in and cooperate. However, during the entire affair he uttered only two words: "More weight."[47] In this way, Giles Corey died on September 19, 1692.

Corey's case marked the only instance in the history of the Massachusetts Bay Colony in which pressing was employed. However, that did not make his surviving relatives feel any better. In fact, the entire incident had a sort of unsettling effect on much of the population. Like the Reverend Burroughs's recital of the Lord's Prayer on Gallows Hill, the cruel killing of Giles Corey made many Puritans wonder if justice was truly being served in the ongoing witch hunt and trials.

To help keep that hunt from losing steam, one of the parties with a strong stake in it, Thomas Putnam, quickly presented new evidence to one of the judges. According to Putnam, on the day of Corey's death, a large group of invisible witches tried to press his daughter, Ann, to death. Then, the girl had been visited by a friendly spirit, which told her that Corey's death was deserved and that, because of it, Ann would be spared. Though this story, clearly manufactured by the elder Putnam, soothed some members of the community, others were not convinced. Cracks were beginning to form in the wall of hysteria that had cut Salem off from the world of reason, justice, and mercy. Soon, that deadly wall would collapse completely, leading to the end of the trials.

Chapter Six

SKEPTICISM LEADS TO THE END

Eventually, the hysteria faded, and people began to grow skeptical of the harsh punishments that the accused were facing. Giles Corey's accidental execution began to open the eyes of many Puritans in Salem to the falseness of their claims. On September 22, eight more people were hanged at Gallows Hill. Though many people continued on insisting that the accusations were real, many in the community had begun to face the harsh realization that these deaths were the result of a very well manufactured lie. Several factors led to this realization. However, the death of Giles Corey helped begin the process of surfacing the truth.

One man partly responsible for the beginning of the end of the Salem witch trials was a local scholar named Thomas Brattle. He was among the higher educated people of the community, and once he voiced his concern that these

trials all stemmed from the elaborate lies and imaginations of a few young girls, the community began to listen. "Many of these afflicted persons," he wrote,

who have scores of strange fits in a day, yet in the intervals of time [in between] are hale and hearty ... as though nothing had afflicted them ... Furthermore, these afflicted persons do say ... that they can see specters when their eyes are shut ... I am sure they lie, [or] at least speak falsely ... for [this] is an utter impossibility. It is true, they may strongly fancy, or have things represented in their imaginations when their eyes are shut. And I think this is all that ought to be allowed to these blind, nonsensical girls.[48]

Brattle was among one of the first to

Afflicted Girls Cannot Be Trusted

In his long public statement released on October 8, 1692, the noted English intellectual Thomas Brattle disputed the evidence presented in the witch trials and suggested that the accusations of the afflicted girls could not be trusted. He also pointed out, in this passage, that many of the executed persons seemed innocent when facing their deaths:

> In the opinion of many unprejudiced, considerate, and considerable spectators, some of the condemned went out of the world not only with great protestations, but also with good shows of innocency … They protested their innocency as in the presence of the great God, whom forthwith they were to appear before. They wished … that their blood might be the last innocent blood shed upon that account. With great affection [emotion], they entreated Mr. Cotton Mather to pray with them. They prayed that God would discover what witchcrafts were among us. They forgave their accusers … They prayed earnestly for pardon for all other sins … and [they] seemed to be very sincere, upright, and sensible of their circumstances.[1]

1. Quoted in Frances Hill, ed., *The Salem Witch Trials Reader*. New York, NY: Da Capo, 2000, pp. 91–92.

blatantly say that the girls orchestrated these deaths with events that transpired simply in their imagination. After this public attempt at reason, many people in the community began to agree with him.

Suspicion of Witchcraft Ceased

Brattle found that he was not alone in holding suspect the honesty and integrity of the girls' accusations and testimony. The accusations continued after the September 22 hangings, increasing both in number and outrageousness. The number of those accused by Abigail Williams rose to about 57. Meanwhile, an accused witch claimed she had attended a meeting involving 25 witches, and someone else said that there were more than 300 witches in the colony. In the midst of the hysteria, an Andover man, William Barker, reported that Satan was planning to destroy all the churches in Massachusetts and replace worship of God with worship of the devil. By October 1, 1692, about 150 accused witches were sitting in colonial jails, and at least another 200 had been accused of witchcraft but were not yet arrested because there was no more room in those jails.

It was not simply the numbers of suspected witches that had begun to strain believability. It was also who was being accused. Throughout most of the witch hunt, hearings, and trials, the vast majority of suspects had been poor, or at least of modest means, and also socially and politically powerless. However, in late September and early October, the afflicted girls began accusing people of much higher standing in the community. The mother-in-law of magistrate Jonathan Corwin was accused of being a witch, for instance. Also accused were the two sons of a well-respected former governor, Simon Bradstreet, and the wife of the Reverend John Hale, one of the most distinguished churchmen in New England. Finally, Lady Mary Phips, wife of the present governor, William Phips, was publicly accused of practicing witchcraft. It is revealing that none of these people were arrested, nor were the accusations against them taken seriously, even for a moment. Clearly, the supposedly afflicted girls had finally gone too far.

Historians have pointed out that the girls and other accusers had made two fundamental mistakes. First, there were simply too many witches. It was one thing to accuse a few members of society of being evil agents of the devil; it was quite another to claim that the colony was literally riddled with hundreds or thousands of witches. Even the most gullible and religiously devout members of the community began to see that such claims had to be excessive and therefore the accusers themselves could not be trusted.

Second, in their youthful ignorance, vanity, and frenzied attempt to exert power over their society, the girls eventually thought they could bring down the rich and powerful people who ran that society. However, this was self-delusion. As has been true time after time in history, those in power could not be easily dislodged from their high positions. As soon as they and their families were threatened by the widening hysteria, the trials suddenly came to a halt. On October 29, Phips ordered that imprisonment of people suspected of witchcraft must cease, and he also officially shut down the court of Oyer and Terminer. The Salem witch trials were, for all intents and purposes, over.

Releasing the Accused

Though the witchcraft trials had ended, the local jails were still full of people who had been accused of evil doings. The dilemma the governor and other community leaders now faced was what to do with these prisoners. At first, the officials were reluctant simply to release them all. After all, what if some of them were indeed witches? The fact that the afflicted girls had gone too far by accusing Lady Phips of being a witch did not necessarily indicate that all of the earlier accusations had been wrong.

Province of the Massachusetts-Bay.

AN ACT,

Made and Passed by the Great and General Court or Assembly of Her Majesty's Province of the Massachusetts-Bay in **New-England**, Held at **Boston** the 17th Day of **October**, 1711.

Nat Lambert Salen

Jan 28 1808

An Act to Reverse the Attainders of *George Burroughs* and others for Witchcraft.

FORASMUCH *as in the Year of our Lord One Thousand Six Hundred Ninety Two, Several Towns within this Province were Infested with a horrible Witchcraft or Possession of Devils ; And at a Special Court of Oyer and Terminer holden at Salem, in the County of* Essex *in the same Year* One Thousand Six Hundred Ninety Two, George Burroughs *of Wells,* John Procter, George Jacob, John Willard, Giles Core, *and his Wife,* Rebecca Nurse, *and* Sarah Good, *all of Salem aforesaid :* Elizabeth How, *of Ipswich,* Mary Eastey, Sarah Wild *and* Abigail Hobbs *all of Topsfield :* Samuel Wardell, Mary Parker, Martha Carrier, Abigail Falkner, Anne Foster, Rebecca Eames, Mary Post, *and* Mary Lacey, *all of Andover :* Mary Bradbury *of Salisbury :* and Dorcas Hoar *of Beverly ; Were severally Indicted, Convicted and Attained of Witchcraft, and some of them put to Death, Others lying still under the like Sentence of the said Court, and liable to have the same Executed upon them.*

A   **The**

This official document from 1713 essentially states that each party mentioned in it should be absolved of the accusation that they were witches.

The solution seemed to be to create a new court, which was called the Superior Court of Judicature. Its mandate would be not to try new witches, but to decide which of the prisoners could safely be released and which should remain in custody. The expectation was that the new court would be much fairer than the earlier one because no spectral evidence would be allowed. Indeed, without the girls' testimony that they saw invisible beings harassing them and others, little other convincing evidence of witchcraft remained. Therefore, when 56 prisoners were tried by the new court in January 1693, 53 had their cases speedily dismissed. The other three people were found guilty, mainly because they had confessed to being witches.

Though by law the three convicted people were subject to the death penalty, they were never executed. Governor Phips granted them pardons, saying, "Considering how the matter had been [so badly] managed [in the previous trials], I sent a reprieve, whereby the execution was stopped." Furthermore, Phips stated that he wanted to eliminate

the black cloud that threatened this province with destruction. For ... this delusion of the devil did spread and its effects touched the lives and estates of many of their Majesty's subjects and [the] reputations of some of the principal persons here, and indeed unhappily clogged and interrupted their Majesty's affairs, which has been a great vexation to me.[49]

Trying to put the colony's troubles in the past and restore a semblance of order and justice, in May 1693, Phips granted pardons to all those still held in the jails. Even those who had escaped confinement by fleeing the colony were pardoned. This meant the fugitives could safely come home and the authorities could begin freeing those who were still behind bars.

Formal Acceptance

In spite of the governor's pardons, however, emptying the prisons was not a simple matter. This is because under the colony's laws, prisoners were financially responsible for their own upkeep while confined in jail. Only those who could afford it, or whose relatives could afford it, could obtain release. "Criminals were not coddled in these days," Marion L. Starkey explained,

nor were those on whom the merest shadow of suspicion had ever rested. You did not in prison become the guest of the state. [Instead] you paid your way. Even if you were wholly innocent, if it were proved that you had been wrongly deprived of your liberty, you still could not leave until you had reimbursed the jailer for his expenditures in your behalf, the food he had fed you, the shackles he had placed on your wrists and ankles. Prices varied slightly at the various prisons, but in general board averaged about two shillings and sixpence a week. Some of the *witches had been running up a bill at this rate for more than a year ... Farms had to be mortgaged to raise the ransom, and they were often farms already impoverished by the half-hearted attention they had had while the trials monopolized everyone's time and attention.*[50]

As a result of these unpleasant realities, some people were forced to remain in jail well after they had been pardoned. A few, including an elderly woman named Sarah Daston, wasted away and died in captivity, abandoned to their sad fate by family, friends, and society. Inmate Mary Watkins managed to get out only after a Virginia planter paid her prison bills in exchange for her working for several years as his indentured servant. Meanwhile, another imprisoned woman, Margaret Jacobs, had the good fortune to have a kindly local citizen pay her way to freedom; she was expected to pay him back but only at a rate that she could manage comfortably. The two pregnant women convicted of being witches, Elizabeth Proctor and Abigail Faulkner, were not so lucky. They had their babies in jail, and when they finally got out, they were scorned by most people and experienced both social rejection and poverty for many years to come.

Though the trials ended and the prisons eventually emptied, justice was not immediately served in the cases of most who had been drawn into the nightmare of witchcraft hysteria. However, that did not stop many of these wronged people from seeking justice, even when it took years to achieve it. In 1693, not long after Governor Phips issued his pardons, several of the released prisoners applied to the colonial government for restitution of their confiscated property. These petitions were summarily ignored. However, the injured parties persisted. Although the General Court declared the trials unlawful in 1702, there was still work to be done. In 1709, many of the people who had suffered because of the trials submitted a petition calling for the legal reversal of all convictions in the witch trials, including those of the people who had been executed. Finally, in 1711, a bill passed reversing all the former convictions. The government also paid financial restitution to the families of many of the victims.

Reverend Parris's Downfall

In this way, at least a few of the wrongs suffered by the victims of the trials were eventually righted. However, what about justice for those who had perpetrated the hysteria and the death and misery it had caused? With much disdain and anger, many of the victims and their families remembered the key role played by Reverend Parris, who had stirred up much of the hysteria through his incendiary sermons warning that witches lurked at every turn. They also remembered the roles played by the judges who had so gullibly taken the word of hysterical, attention-seeking children over that of responsible adults with unblemished

An Attempt at Compensation

A mong the petitions for financial restitution brought before the Massachusetts government was this one by Isaac Esty, the husband of one of the accused witches, Mary Esty:

Isaac Esty of Topsfield in the county of Essex ... having been sorely [treated] through the holy [and] awful providence of God depriving him of his beloved wife Mary Esty, who suffered death in the year 1692 [and] under the fearful odium of one of the worst of crimes that can be laid to the charge of mankind, as if she had been guilty of witchcraft ... [I] am firmly persuaded that she was innocent ... Upon consideration of a notification from the Honored [General] Court desiring [myself and] others under the like circumstances to give some account of [how much] my estate was [financially damaged] by reason of such a hellish molestation, [I] do hereby declare ... that my wife was near upon 5 months imprisoned, all which time I provided maintenance for her at my own cost [and] charge, went constantly twice [a week] to provide for her what she needed ... [and] I was constrained to be at the charge of transporting her to [and] fro. So that I [can not] but think my charge in time and money might amount to 20 pounds besides my trouble [and] sorrow of heart in being deprived of her after such a manner which this world can never make me any compensation for.[1]

1. Quoted in "Petitions for Compensation and Decision Concerning Compensation, 1710–1711." Salem Witchcraft Trials, 1692, Famous American Trials. www.law.umkc.edu/faculty/projects/ftrials/salem/SAL_PET.HTM.

reputations. Additionally, there were the roles played by those very children, the girls who had started all the trouble in the first place. It seemed only fair that these individuals should have to pay some kind of price for their failings.

In at least some cases, the key perpetrators did suffer some kind of negative consequences. In the months following the end of the trials, for instance, Reverend Parris encountered the wrath of many in his congregation who held him partly responsible for the witch hunt. Early in 1697, a group of these Salem Village worshippers attempted to void his salary. "His believing the

Reverend Parris is shown here trying to force a man into a confession.

devil's accusations," they said, "and readily departing from all charity to persecute the blameless and godly [citizens] are just causes for our refusal [to pay him]."[51] Parris fought back for a while, but over time, more and more villagers refused to set foot in church while he was still the minister. In 1697, he finally resigned and left town, taking young Betty with him. The new village minister, Joseph Green, eventually restored order in the church, and reinstated many whom Parris had expelled at the height of the witchcraft hysteria.

Most of the judges who had served in the court of Oyer and Terminer did not suffer the kind of social rejection that Reverend Parris did. However, one of their number, Samuel Sewall, did end up atoning for his role in the fiasco. In January 1697, Sewall released a statement that a local minister recited from the pulpit. Amounting to a confession of guilt, it read in part:

> As to the guilt contracted upon the opening of the late commission [court] of Oyer and Terminer in Salem ... [I, Samuel Sewall] desire to take the blame and shame of it, asking pardon of men, and especially desiring prayers that God ... would pardon that sin and all [my] other sins.[52]

Apologies Accepted?

As for the young girls whose secret playing with magic, fits, and incriminating accusations had largely driven the witch hunt, most were never punished for causing such misery. A few, including Betty Parris, Mercy Lewis, and Mary Walcott, did eventually marry, although little is known about their later lives. Only one of the girls, Ann Putnam, ever publicly expressed remorse for what she had done. In 1706, Ann penned a confession and gave it to Reverend Green to read to his congregation in Salem Village. "I desire to be humbled before God," it began,

> for that sad and humbling providence that befell my father's family in the year about [1692]; that I, then being in my childhood, should, by such a providence of God, be made an instrument for the accusing of several persons of a grievous crime, whereby their lives were taken away from them, whom now I have just grounds and good reason to believe they were innocent persons; and that it was a great delusion of Satan that deceived me in that sad time, whereby I justly fear I have been instrumental, with others, though ignorantly and unwittingly, to bring upon myself and this land the guilt of innocent blood ... Particularly, as I was a chief instrument of accusing of Goodwife Nurse and her two sisters, I desire to lie in the dust, and to be humbled for it, in that I was a cause, with others, of

The girls at the center of the Salem witch trials did not face formal punishment for the lives they ruined with their accusations.

so sad a calamity to them and their families; for which … [I] earnestly beg forgiveness of God, and from all those unto whom I have given just cause of sorrow and offence.[53]

The members of Reverend Green's congregation generously forgave her and allowed her to join them. However, there were many in Salem, including some who had lived through the witch hunt as well as their children who were born later, who refused to accept such apologies after the fact. In their view, repentance, though admirable, could not bring back dead loved ones or restore ruined family reputations.

One of those who held grudges all their lives was Philip English, a Salem merchant whose wife, Mary, had been accused of witchcraft, rudely dragged from her bed, and thrown into jail. (She was later released.) For decades following the trials, English loudly denounced all the former authority figures who had run them, including the Reverend Nicholas Noyes. On several occasions over the years, English was arrested for slander and spent the night in jail. However, his anger over the treatment of his wife and the brutal, untimely deaths of his friends John Proctor and Rebecca Nurse never subsided. On his deathbed in 1736, English was urged to finally forgive Noyes, who had died several years before. Among English's last words were "I'll be damned if I forgive him!"[54]

REMEMBERING THE TRIALS

The effects of the Salem witch trials were felt long after the end of the trials. Lessons were learned and things were subsequently avoided after the hysteria that took the lives of many during that fateful year in Salem, Massachusetts. These events showed people for years to come what can happen when an entire community is filled with fear and feeds into absurd beliefs without first consulting reason and objectivity. It is obvious that one of the main driving forces in the story of life after the trials was the sheer fact that no one wanted such a ridiculous and completely avoidable event to be repeated. Several laws were passed among colonial societies that essentially prohibited the use of baseless accusations to lead to a trial and prosecution. The acts stemming from this time helped mold the U.S. judicial system into the balanced, respectable, and functional body that it is today.

Modern Salem

It was inevitable that the history of the Salem witch trials would spark interest among people in both past and present cultures. Immediately following the trials, it was evident that the community did not want their mistakes widely spread and talked about. Visitors interested in seeing the place where the trials and executions took place were not welcome, and questions were not answered.

However, long after the hysteria settled, people of Salem realized the profitable possibilities of accepting the town's history and began marketing the town as a tourist attraction. Modern Salem is visited by a very extensive population of witch trial enthusiasts. These enthusiasts can explore the Salem Witch Museum, which began educating visitors in 1972. This museum presents the story of the

The Salem Witch Museum is a very popular spot with tourists visiting the village.

Shown here is the memorial to the Salem witch trials that can be seen in Danvers, Massachusetts.

IN MEMORY OF THOSE INNOCENTS
WHO DIED DURING THE
SALEM VILLAGE WITCHCRAFT HYSTERIA
OF 1692

Each of the 20 benches that make up the Salem Witch Trials Memorial is inscribed with one of the names of the victims.

trials through exhibits and multimedia presentations. It is Salem's most visited museum.

The abstract idea of witches has become a part of Salem's heritage, and many businesses and public sectors around town emphasize the history of the trials, which is evident in their marketing practices. For example, the local fire and police department have a witch as their logo, and the school's mascot is portrayed as a witch. Not surprisingly, Halloween is the most popular time in Salem for tourism and events, and several community members and tourists dress up for most of October. There was a memorial dedicated for the 300th anniversary of the trials in 1992, which also proves to be a common place for tourists to visit. The memorial consists of a large stone wall to commemorate the lives of the accused witches. Quotes from protests of the victims, taken directly from court documents, are inscribed on the entryway of the memorial. Twenty granite benches inscribed with names of the victims also stand at the memorial in honor of the lives lost during those tragic months in Salem in 1692.

Modern Adaptations

Much like many events in history, modern adaptations of the story began to be created. One of these is particularly notable—*The Crucible*, written by Arthur Miller in 1952, is a theatrical adaptation of the Salem witch trials. This play takes the facts of the Salem trials and turns them into a fictional portrayal of the events that took place in 1692. Parallels were drawn by Miller to relevant events happening in 1952, and his play became something of a warning as a result.

During the time that *The Crucible* was composed, the events of the McCarthy hearings were beginning to unfold. These hearings were the result of U.S. Senator Joseph McCarthy accusing several Americans of being Communists. These accusations, much like the hysteria of the Salem witch trials, snowballed quickly and created chaos. Many lives were ruined—often people not even remotely associated with the Communist Party. However, in the same fashion as the witch trials, the accusations built up, and with them, so did the fear and ignorance that led to widespread hysteria and the prosecution of innocent people. Though the play was written about the Salem witch trials, it was meant to parallel the current events, hopefully opening the eyes of those who did not see how close history was to repeating itself.

Miller discussed these parallels and his reasons for writing *The Crucible* in an article published in *The New Yorker*, on October 21, 1996—nearly 50 years after the play was created. He stated,

The Crucible *was an act of desperation. Much of my desperation branched out, I suppose, from a typical Depression-era trauma—the blow struck on the mind by the rise of European Fascism and the brutal anti-Semitism it had brought to power. But by 1950, when I began to think of writing about the hunt for Reds [Communists] in America, I was motivated in some great part by the paralysis that had set in among many liberals who, despite their discomfort with the inquisitors' violations of civil rights, were fearful, and with good reason, of being identified as covert Communists if they should protest too strongly.*[55]

The Crucible is still a popular play today, and it continues to remind audiences and readers of the dangers of giving in to fear and unreasonable suspicion.

Miller's play suggests that fear, as the driving force of both parallel events, is a force that still continues to crumble our societies' values. The people of Salem in 1692 accused others of witchcraft out of a sense of fear that if they did not, they themselves would be denounced, just as people in the 1950s accused others of being Communists under the assumption that they could be an accuser, instead of the accused. The parable of the Salem witch trials proves to be relevant in modern culture, just as it was in the past. Without education, reason, and individuality, irrational fear and paranoia set in, leaving otherwise outlandish ideals as the only thing people cling to for reassurance.

The Story Continues

It took more than 300 years, but another important step on the road to healing after the tragedy of the Salem witch trials was taken in 2001. That year, the Massachusetts government officially exonerated, or cleared the names of, five women who were hanged for the crime of witchcraft in 1692. These five women were Bridget Bishop (the first woman sentenced in 1692), Susannah Martin, Alice Parker, Wilmot Redd, and Margaret Scott.

Another important development in the quest to tell the full story of the Salem witch trials occurred in 2016. In January of that year, scholars identified the exact location of the hangings that took place during the witch trials. The location was a spot on the lower slope of Gallows Hill, which is now known as Proctor's Ledge. This discovery ended centuries of speculating and added another level of closure to the story. Now, people can visit Proctor's Ledge and pay their respects to the victims at the exact location where

they died. Work is currently being planned for a formal memorial to be built at the site.

Learning from the Past

The enduring legacy of the Salem witch trials is what they taught us about the danger of letting fear become stronger than reason, especially in matters of government and law. At times throughout American history, hysteria has led to injustice, especially for minority groups. When this happens, the memory of the Salem witch trials is sometimes invoked to remind people of what can happen when we let false accusations rooted in fear ruin innocent lives.

The McCarthy hearings are perhaps the best-known example of a modern American witch hunt, but they are far from the only example. Controversial stop and frisk laws, which allowed law enforcement officials to stop and search anyone who they believed looked threatening, ultimately targeted black and Latino men more than any other group, with many calling the practice a kind of modern witch hunt rooted in the fear that these races were more prone to violent action. In addition, ever since the terrorist attacks of September 11, 2001, many Muslims living in the United States have been the victims of false accusations and irrational suspicion.

In times of fear and uncertainty, our first instinct is often to look for people to punish and blame. It is easy to give in to fear and to fall into a state of hysteria, but the Salem witch trials taught us that this way leads to chaos and injustice. Americans must continue to learn from the dark events of the past, such as the Salem witch trials, and work hard to ensure that history does not repeat itself.

Notes

Introduction:
A History Based on False Accusations

1. Frances Hill, ed., *The Salem Witch Trials Reader*. New York, NY: Da Capo, 2000, p. xvii.

2. Quoted in "The Malleus Maleficarum, Part I." The Malleus Maleficarum of James Sprenger and Heinrich Kramer. www.malleusmaleficarum.org/part_I/mm01_06a.html.

3. James A. Haught, *Holy Horrors*. New York, NY: Prometheus, 1990, pp. 75–76.

4. Haught, *Holy Horrors*, p. 76.

5. Hill, *The Salem Witch Trials Reader*, p. 3.

Chapter One:
The Strong Beliefs That Led to Chaos

6. Richard Weisman, *Witchcraft, Magic, and Religion in 17th-Century Massachusetts*. Amherst, MA: University of Massachusetts Press, 1984, p. 26.

7. Marion L. Starkey, *The Devil in Massachusetts: A Modern Enquiry into the Salem Witch Trials*. New York, NY: Random House, 1989, p. 31.

8. Starkey, *The Devil in Massachusetts*, p. 32.

9. Carol F. Karlsen, *The Devil in the Shape of a Woman: Witchcraft in Colonial New England*. Magnolia, MA: Peter Smith, 1999, p. 46.

10. Quoted in Hill, *The Salem Witch Trials Reader*, p. 126.

Chapter Two:
A Blind Following

11. Quoted in "Increase Mather: Remarkable Providences: An Essay for the Recording of Illustrious Providences (Boston, 1684)." Hanover Historical Texts Projects. history.hanover.edu/texts/matherrp.html.

12. Quoted in "Increase Mather."

13. Quoted in Hill, *The Salem Witch Trials Reader*, p. 19.

14. Quoted in Rachel Walker, "Cotton Mather," Salem Witch Trials. www.iath.virginia.edu/salem/people/c_mather.html.

15. Quoted in Hill, *The Salem Witch Trials Reader*, p. 61.

16. Quoted in Hill, *The Salem Witch Trials Reader*, p. 381.

Chapter Three: Public Accusations Lead to Questioning

17. Karlsen, *The Devil in the Shape of a Woman*, p. 45.

18. Starkey, *The Devil in Massachusetts*, p. 49.

19. Starkey, *The Devil in Massachusetts*, p. 51.

20. Starkey, *The Devil in Massachusetts*, p. 51.

21. Quoted in Marilynne K. Roach, *The Salem Witch Trials: A Day-by-Day Chronicle of a Community Under Siege*. New York, NY: Taylor Trade, 2002, p. 25.

22. Stacy Schiff, *The Witches*. New York, NY: Little, Brown and Company, 2015, p. 49.

23. Quoted in Roach, *The Salem Witch Trials*, p. 27.

24. Quoted in Roach, *The Salem Witch Trials*, p. 30.

25. Quoted in Roach, *The Salem Witch Trials*, p. 31.

26. Quoted in Hill, *The Salem Witch Trials Reader*, p. 62.

27. Quoted in Hill, *The Salem Witch Trials Reader*, p. 299.

Chapter Four: The Witches' Fate

28. Quoted in Hill, *The Salem Witch Trials Reader*, p. 102.

29. Quoted in Hill, *The Salem Witch Trials Reader*, p. 101.

30. Roach, *The Salem Witch Trials*, pp. 158–159.

31. Quoted in Chadwick Hansen, *Witchcraft at Salem*. New York, NY: George Braziller, 1985, p. 65.

32. Quoted in George L. Burr, ed., *Narratives of the Witchcraft Cases, 1648–1706*. New York, NY: Barnes and Noble, 1975, p. 352.

33. Quoted in Hansen, *Witchcraft at Salem*, p. 126.

34. Quoted in Frances Hill, *A Delusion of Satan: The Full Story of the*

Salem Witch Trials. New York, NY: Da Capo, 2002, p. 156.

Chapter Five:
Tunnel Vision

35. Quoted in Hill, *The Salem Witch Trials Reader*, p. 77.

36. Quoted in Hill, *The Salem Witch Trials Reader*, pp. 77–78.

37. Quoted in Hill, *A Delusion of Satan*, p. 176.

38. Quoted in Starkey, *The Devil in Massachusetts*, p. 93.

39. Quoted in Starkey, *The Devil in Massachusetts*, p. 94.

40. Quoted in Starkey, *The Devil in Massachusetts*, p. 94.

41. Starkey, *The Devil in Massachusetts*, pp. 94–95.

42. Quoted in "Benjamin Abbot v. Martha Carrier." Electronic Text Center, University of Virginia Library, The Salem Witchcraft Papers, vol. 1. etext.virginia.edu/etcbin/toccernew2?id=BoySal1.sgm&images=images/modeng&data=/texts/english/modeng/oldsalem&tag=public&part=140&division=div2.

43. Quoted in Burr, *Narratives of the Witchcraft Cases*, p. 244.

44. Quoted in Roach, *The Salem Witch Trials*, p. 227.

45. Quoted in Hill, *The Salem Witch Trials Reader*, pp. 194–195.

46. Quoted in Roach, *The Salem Witch Trials*, p. 77.

47. Quoted in Roach, *The Salem Witch Trials*, p. 297.

Chapter Six:
Skepticism Leads to the End

48. Quoted in Hill, *The Salem Witch Trials Reader*, p. 98.

49. Quoted in Burr, *Narratives of the Witchcraft Cases*, p. 201.

50. Starkey, *The Devil in Massachusetts*, p. 230.

51. Quoted in Starkey, *The Devil in Massachusetts*, p. 250.

52. Quoted in M.H. Thomas, ed., *The Diary of Samuel Sewall*. New York, NY: Farrar, Straus, and Giroux, 1973, p. 97.

53. Quoted in Matthew Dennis, Department of History, University of Oregon, "Ann Putnam's Confession (1706)."

www.uoregon.edu/~mjdennis/
courses/wk3_putnam.htm.

54. Quoted in Roach, *The Salem Witch Trials*, p. 572.

Epilogue:
Remembering the Trials

55. Arthur Miller, "Why I Wrote 'The Crucible,'" *The New Yorker*. www.newyorker.com/archive/ content/?020422fr_archive02.

For More Information

Books

Boraas, Tracey. *The Salem Witch Trials*. Mankato, MN: Capstone, 2003.
This is an excellent introduction to the weird and frightening trials of witches in Salem for young people.

Hill, Frances. *A Delusion of Satan: The Full Story of the Salem Witch Trials*. New York, NY: Da Capo, 2002.
This well-organized and well-written account of the trials was written by one of the leading authorities on the subject.

Landau, Elaine. *The Salem Witchcraft Trials: Would You Join the Madness?* Berkeley Heights, NJ: Enslow Elementary, 2015.
Landau asks readers to decide what they would do if they had been alive at the time of the Salem witch trials.

Miller, Arthur. *The Crucible: A Play in Four Acts*. New York, NY: Penguin Classics, 2003.
Miller's dramatic adaptation of the Salem witch trials remains the most famous and most studied work of literature about this period in American history.

Schanzer, Rosalyn. *Witches!: The Absolutely True Tale of Disaster in Salem*. Washington, DC: National Geographic, 2011.
Schanzer's account of the Salem witch trials features primary sources and creative illustrations.

Websites

A Brief History of the Salem Witch Trials (www.smithsonianmag. com/history/a-brief-history-of-the-salem-witch-trials-175162489/?no-ist)
This website provides a simplified history of the trials with concrete information and interesting images.

Salem, Massachusetts City Guide (www.salemweb.com/ guide/witches.php)
This is an enlightening overview of the famous town, then and now, with several links to sites with further information about the town and the infamous witch trials.

Salem Witch Museum (www.salemwitchmuseum. com/education)
The website for the most visited museum in Salem features several links and information about the trials' history, as well as information about the museum.

Salem Witch Trials (nationalgeographic.org/ interactive/salem-interactive/)
This interactive site explains the trials' history while also giving visitors an opportunity to engage with the material through games and quizzes.

Salem Witch Trials: The World Behind the Hysteria (school.discoveryeducation. com/schooladventures/ salemwitchtrials/)
This website has information on daily life in Salem at the time of the trials, including what role religion played in daily life and what children did during the day. The website also has a movie on the Salem witch trials and information on key people behind the trials.

**The Witches Curse
(www.pbs.org/wnet/secrets/
witches-curse-
interactive-explore-
salem/1579/)**
This website has a detailed
timeline of the Salem witch
trials, as well as a map with
information about important
buildings and people. It also
includes informative videos
about the Salem witch trials.

Index

of, 47

O

Osborne, Sarah
  accusation of,
    37–38, 40, 43
  death of, 44
  questioning of, 41,
    43
Oyer and Terminer
  court, 52, 54, 75, 81

P

Parris, Elizabeth
  strange behaviors
    of, 27, 29–31, 34,
    36, 57
  in Tituba's circle,
    31–32, 35
Parris, Samuel, 26, 31,
  33, 35–36, 43, 78–81
peine forte et dure
  (punishment hard
  and severe), 70
Phips, William
  commission of Oyer
    and Terminer, 52
  method of trials, 53
  pardons issued by,
    77–78
  trials halted by, 60,
    75
Pilgrims, 18

Plymouth colony, 18
Proctor, Elizabeth, 46,
  63–66, 78
Proctor, John, 46,
  48–49, 63–66, 69, 83
Puritans/Puritanism
  plain living, 20
  social prejudice
    among, 22
  status of women in,
    22
  views on lawyers,
    40
  views on magic, 32
Putnam, Ann, 33,
  37–38, 44, 47, 69, 81
Putnam, John, 47, 59
Putnam, Thomas,
  43–44, 59, 71–72

S

Salem Town, 19–20,
  36, 38, 41, 47, 56
Salem Village
  crimes/punish-
    ments in, 22–24
  culture of, 16
  religious domina-
    tion of, 20
  as tourist spot,
    84–88, 90
Salem witch trials
  appointing court/

judges for, 52–53
courthouse of, 51
early misgivings
  about, 75
evidence admissible
  in, 53–54
legacy of, 84–88, 90
termination of, 75
Salem Witch Trials
  Memorial, 7, 70,
    86–88, 90
Sewall, Samuel, 53, 81
Sheldon, Susan, 33
Sibley, Mary, 36
Sprenger, James, 13
Stacey, William, 54,
  56
Stoughton, William,
  53
Superior Court of
  Judicature, 77

T

Tituba
  accused of witch-
    craft, 37–39, 43
  imprisonment of, 44
  magic and, 31–33
  questioning of,
    43–44, 46
Token for the Children
  of New England
  (Mather), 27

Picture Credits

Cover, pp. 7 (top), 9, 11, 14, 17, 55, 62, 67 Bettmann/Contributor/Bettmann/ Getty Images; pp. 4–5 Ogram/Wikimedia Commons, p. 6 (bottom left) DEA/ G. DAGLI ORTI/Contributor/De Agostini/Getty Images; pp. 6 (bottom right), 45, 68, 76, 80, 82 Everett Historical/Shutterstock.com; p. 6 (top) Georgios Kollidas/ Shuterstock.com; p. 7 (bottom left) Transcendental Graphics/Contributor/Archive Photos/Getty Images; p. 7 (bottom right) Central Press/Stringer/Hulton Archive/ Getty Images; p. 12 Hello world/Wikimedia Commons; p. 19 PawelMM/Wikimedia Commons; p. 21 Ed Clark/Contributor/The LIFE Images Collection/Getty Images; p. 23 Charles Phelps Cushing/ClassicStock/Getty Images; p. 28 NYPL/Science Source/ Getty Images; p. 30 CREATISTA/Shutterstock.com; p. 32 Interim Archives/Contributor/ Archive Photos/Getty Images; p. 37 Scewing/Wikimedia Commons; p. 42 MPI/Stringer/ Archive Photos/Getty Images; p. 47 Maximoalberto/Wikimedia Commons; p. 48 Lee Snider/Getty Images; p. 51 Jerry Cooke/Contributor/The LIFE Images Collection/Getty Images; p. 58 Education Images/Contributor/Universal Images Group/Getty Images; p. 70 Tim1965/Wikimedia Commons; p. 85 JTB Photo/Contributor/Universal Images Group/Getty Images; p. 86 Boston Globe/Contributor/Boston Globe/Getty Images; p. 87 John Burke/Getty Images; p. 89 Robbie Jack - Corbis/Contributor/Corbis Historical/Getty Images.

About the Author

Tanya Dellaccio is a SUNY Fredonia graduate who received her Bachelor of Arts degree in both English and Graphic Design. She currently resides in Buffalo, New York, where she spends her time writing and designing children's books.